W9-BTK-870

Travel Egypt

Nile Cruise

A GUIDE TO AN EGYPTIAN HOLIDAY

Written and Researched by

Janet Wood

Travel Egypt Series on the Internet

www.ancientnile.co.uk and www.worldthroughthelens.com

This book is dedicated to my parents, Cyril and Jean Holmes

No part of this book may be reproduced in any form without the prior permission from the publisher except for the use of a brief passage in a review. All Rights Reserved.

The right of Janet Wood to be identified as the author, designer and illustrator of this work has been asserted by her in accordance with the Copyright, Designs and Patents Act 1988. All illustrations and photographs published in this book are copyrighted by Michael & Janet Wood.

At the time of going to press the third party website URLs displayed in the text of this book were available on the Internet. The publisher is not responsible for the content of these third party websites (including without limitation, outdated, inaccurate, or incomplete information) and access to any such site is at the user's own risk.

The publisher and author have done their best to ensure the accuracy and currency of all the information in Travel Egypt; Nile Cruise, however they can accept no responsibility for any loss, injury, or inconvenience sustained by any traveller as a result of information or advice contained in this guide. The opinions passed are the author's own and as such are subjective and personal to that individual and therefore may not coincide with your own experiences.

This book is subject to revision when deemed necessary by the publisher or author. Front and back cover design by Janet Wood.

This 1st Edition paperback published in Great Britain © February 2006 by M J Wood Digital Media, Greater Manchester, England

Travel Egypt Series: Nile Cruise, Around Luxor, Photographing the Ancient Sites and a Travel Pack containing all three.

ISBN 0-9548049-4-5   A catalogue record for this book is available from the British Library. Printed by Lightning Source Inc.

CONTENTS

Introduction

One of the questions I am regularly asked with regards to Egyptian travel is, 'What actually happens on a Egyptian Cruise?' So with this in mind I have written this book in order to go through what, in my experience, are the typical events of a Nile holiday. My intention is that hopefully by the time you have finished reading you will have a far better idea of what to expect.

In order to ensure accuracy this book is based solely on my own personal experience. And although I have written the book from the perspective of a UK traveller, over 99% of the information provided will be relevant to most tourists visiting Egypt. As well as covering the basic issues, I will also tell you, 'how it is', and not just romanticise the experience.

Whilst this book contains information on the various sites regularly visited by the cruise ships, it is actually more concerned with general and practical information that you will be hard pressed to find elsewhere, especially in one place.

Obviously I can not guarantee that I will have included all the sites, events, and entertainment that will be made available to you during your stay in Egypt, or that they will happen in the order I have written.

For example, one tour company may include a visit to 'The Workers Village' on the west bank and a perfume shop in Luxor, whilst another may choose Medinet Habu and a papyrus factory.

Each tour company set their own agenda, but generally speaking all the major sites I have mentioned are usually covered at some stage during your holiday.

Whilst a Nile cruise may not give you a fully comprehensive look at Ancient Egypt, is does allow the visitor to get a taste of some of the best sites in a short time, and at a budget price. Besides, if a Nile cruise was good enough for pharaoh, then a luxury cruise must surely be good enough for us mere mortals!

Typical Nile cruise boat

Due to security reasons, the longer cruises from Cairo to Aswan are no longer available. There are a few cruises on Lake Nasser but these only visit the monuments in the old Nubian region, such as Abu Simbel. Therefore, as the most popular cruises start at Luxor, some 315 miles south of Cairo, and travel south to Aswan I have concentrated on these. Luxor actually houses over seventy percent of ancient Egypt's artefacts and sites, so it's a very good place to start your voyage of discovery.

Life goes on much as it did thousands of years ago.

As you leisurely cruise along, the natural beauty of the Nile can take your breath away. With the desert always in the background, life along the River Nile goes on much as it did in the days of the great Pharaohs, with villagers working the land, rearing livestock and fishing the river.

There are more than 300 cruise boats on the Nile, many of which are five-star rated offering trips of various durations including three, four or seven nights. These cruises are a mix of conducted tours, delicious food, coddled relaxation, luxury travel, fantastic sunsets and romantic scenery. So enjoy!

Many years ago a Nile cruise was my first introduction to Egypt and it whetted my appetite so much so that I couldn't wait to get back the following year to see the pyramids and 'Tutankhamun's treasures' at the Museum of Antiquities. Of course, you could always include a stay at Cairo as part of your holiday package, either before or after the cruise. However your itinerary will become much more hectic and the price of your holiday will increase as it will involve an internal air flight between Luxor and Cairo. One year I incorporated Cairo, Luxor and the Red Sea into a 10-day holiday, which was very tiring. It's not too bad if you are fairly young and physically fit but the older you are, the more you will probably feel the hectic pace.

You will find that there are many online travel agencies who are more than happy to offer package holidays, tailor-made vacations (fitted around your needs), specialist tours, or all-inclusive stays. You can find links to both UK and US travel companies offering Egyptian holidays and other worldwide destinations in the links at the end of this book. However for your convenience I have added a direct link below.

http://www.ancientnile.co.uk/eb-links/uk-us-travel.php

Arrival

You will arrive in Luxor either via an International flight, or, if you have already spent some time in Egypt, on an internal Egyptair flight.

At present, departure flights from the UK to Luxor are on Wednesday mornings from either Manchester or Gatwick. People returning back to the UK board the same planes around 5pm, arriving back in England around 10pm. Regarding the US, some flights do fly direct non-stop to Egypt, whilst others fly via a European stop-off, such as London or Frankfurt. You will need to check at the time of booking.

Tourist visas for Egypt can be obtained upon arrival in Egypt for citizens of most countries, including the UK. You will also need a passport that is valid for at least six months and with at least one blank page.

As you enter the terminal you will be handed a visa form, which you will need to complete with your name, address, age, passport, country, flight number etc. The visa will then be checked and stamped, usually at the Bureau de Change counter. The present 30-day tourist visa costs £20 (35US$/ 29 Euros) and usually they will ask that you pay for it with your national currency, i.e. UK Sterling, US dollars, Australian pounds. This is because Egypt is a relatively closed economy, which means they limit the amount of Egyptian currency you can bring into the country but there are no restrictions on the amount of 'foreign' currency you can take in. You will also need to complete an entry card, which will be checked by passport control. Your passport will then be stamped.

I have included a money conversion chart in the final section of this book for GBP, USD, CAD, EURO and AUD currencies, which were correct at the time of writing. However as the exchange rate constantly changes you should use this only as a rough guide. I would suggest that you check the current exchange rate just before you leave for your holiday and add your own up-to-date chart on one of the blank pages I have provided at the end of the book.

The currency in Egypt is Egyptian pounds, expressed locally as LE, which stands for 'livre égyptienne'. There are 100 piastres in 1 Egyptian pound. However as a tourist you are unlikely to see any of these coins.

After passing through passport control and collecting your luggage, you will be met by your travel representative who will arrange for you to be taken by coach to your Nile cruise ship. This should take approximately 20 minutes.

You may find that some of the airport staff and locals may try to get money off you as you're being checked through the airport, usually after they have just flattered you regarding the beauty of your partner. Do not be taken in by this (even if your partner is beautiful ☺) and politely refuse to hand over any money. By the end of your holiday this will have become second nature to you!

If you want to use a luggage trolley you will be charged 2 Egyptian pounds for the privilege. If your bags are not too heavy, or have wheels, I would suggest that you do not bother as the coaches are usually parked just outside the main doors, a distance of some 100 yards.

There will also be a number of unofficial luggage handlers waiting outside, eager to carry your bags to the coach, even to the point of trying to grab them from your hand in their eagerness to 'earn' a fee. If you do not want their help, be firm and say, no (La'a). If you do use their service expect to pay LE2. If you have no Egyptian money, you can offer sterling, but they will expect at least a £1 coin (LE10).

In one instance I saw a fellow tourist offer a 20p UK coin (LE2) to one handler who had more or less snatched the bag from his hand and carried it a mere 20 yards. But the 'luggage handler' rebuffed the offer as an insult even though the tourist had not asked for his services in the first place. A word of warning, do not expect change if you do not have the correct money. Personally, I would not bother with their offers of 'help' unless there is a specific need.

Once you find your coach your bags will be loaded on to it by the driver, if you wish you could offer him a tip, but it is not necessary as your travel company is paying him for his services.

Once on board the boat you will most likely be asked to hand in your passports as part of the Egyptian security measures, this will be returned to you a few days later.

Depending upon your time of arrival, you will be asked to join your rep's welcoming meeting either that day, or the following morning. I would strongly suggest that you attend as during this get-together you will be given general information about the week ahead such as; timetable, boat amenities, hints and tips etc. Plus, you will also be given the opportunity to book additional excursions that may not have been included in your holiday price. These will be presented quite enthusiastically as the travel reps are usually on commission. However this is not to say that they are not good value for money. If this is your first visit to Egypt and you would like to see more than your basic package includes then I would suggest you consider booking some of the extra trips.

By far the most popular extra excursions taken by tourists on a cruise or a stay in Luxor are;

1. Light and Sound Shows at Karnak and Philae Temples.
2. Trip to Abu Simbel.
3. Balloon flight over the Valley of the Kings. (Usually available to those who are also spending a few days in a hotel as part of their holiday)

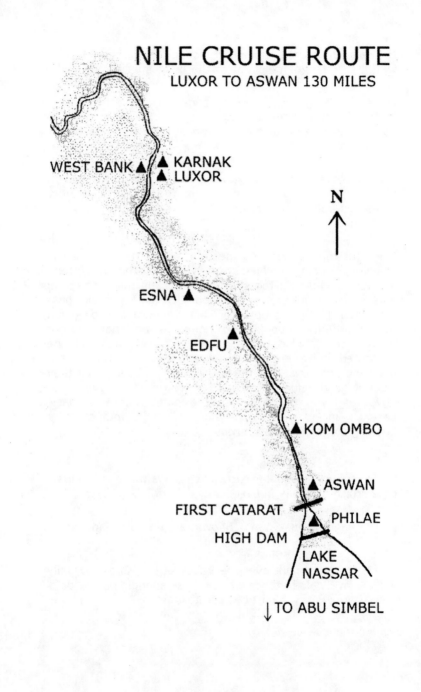

NILE CRUISE ROUTE
LUXOR TO ASWAN 130 MILES

N

WEST BANK ▲ ▲ KARNAK
          ▲ LUXOR

ESNA ▲

EDFU ▲

▲ KOM OMBO

▲ ASWAN

FIRST CATARAT

PHILAE ▲

HIGH DAM

LAKE NASSAR

↓ TO ABU SIMBEL

Typical Nile Cruise Schedule

Day One

Your first morning will be an early start and you will most likely cross over to the West Bank of the River Nile on the first of your inclusive excursions. The travel company will provide guides on all the tours and you usually get split into groups of about twenty to thirty.

Quite often the guides are Egyptologists, or university students studying Egyptology or Archaeology so they are usually very informative and quite witty. However, sometimes you may have a little trouble understanding their accent.

Valley of the Kings

The Valley of the Kings trip usually includes three tomb visits; usually taken in the company of your guide. It's strange to think that in antiquity, some 2000 years ago, the tombs were a top tourist attraction even then! Many of the tomb walls and roofs are covered with hieroglyphs, deities, and painted with a profusion of colours that have survived for thousands of years.

However an optional visit to Tutankhamun's Tomb will cost you extra - approximately £8 at the time of writing. Oh yes, you have to pay more to see his lordship's tomb!

To my surprise many people do actually decide against going into Tutankhamun's tomb and I even heard one guide discouragingly remark, 'It's not worth the money and pretty boring as tombs go.'

Personally, I think he just wanted to get away as soon as possible, knowing there are always long queues for the tomb. In my opinion, it may not be as grand, or as intriguing as some of the other tombs in the valley, but do you really want to have travelled all that way and not see the most famous site in the Valley of the Kings?

Entrance to Pharaoh Tutankhamun's tomb (KV62) in the Valley of the Kings

Tomb Tip 1: You are not allowed videos or cameras in Tutankhamun's tomb and when I last visited all bags containing valuable photographic equipment had to be given to the guardians in charge of the tomb. These were then just piled up together until your return. You were not given any sort of ticket to identify your own bags, so in your absence, anyone could have quite easily taken your belongings.

Unless things change in the future a possible solution to this problem is;

- If you are travelling with a fellow companion I would suggest that you go into the tomb one at a time, so the other person can look after the bags.

- If travelling alone but in a tour group, I would ask one of your fellow tourists if they would kindly look after your personal items.

Tomb Tip 2: If you are in reasonable health, don't mind heights, do not suffer from claustrophobia or a bad back, then one of my favourite tombs to visit is that of Tuthmoses III (KV no.34).

It is situated quite some distance off the main track, in a narrow gorge and is certainly not an easy option, especially in the baking heat. But if you decide to give it ago you will feel as if you have achieved something. However be warned; the entrance lies some 30 metres above ground, and can only be reached by climbing a metal staircase.

Tuthmoses III Tomb (Looking up and down)

Once inside you descend down steep corridors and stairways, which involve some bending before you finally reach the oval shaped burial chamber, reminiscent of a cartouche.

The walls are decorated with scenes from the Book of Amduat that represents the twelve hours of the night and the journey Pharaoh has to undergo in order to reach the

13

Afterlife. The Book of Amduat is the oldest amongst the tomb texts transcribed from the Valley of the Kings.

Inside KV34, Tuthmoses III tomb

Tomb Tip 3: Flash photography is not allowed in any tomb interior so camera shake is always going to be a problem due to long exposure. One way around this is to rest your camera firmly against a tomb wall, or on the floor, whilst taking the photo. Also, if possible, reduce your depth of field in order to further reduce the exposure time. Internal photography without flash and tripod is always tricky, but not impossible. You can read more about what to photograph in our 'Photographing the Ancient Sites' book which is available from our website, www.ancientnile.co.uk.

Note: You can no longer purchase photography tickets, which allow you to take non-flash photography inside the tombs. The reason behind this is baffling, as non-flash photography does not harm the delicate artwork. I can only assume it is to encourage tourists to purchase photographs or postcards from the local traders.

At present, if you are travelling with an organised group then your chances of taking interior tomb photographs are zero. However, if you are travelling independently, or if you get a few minutes to explore on your own at the end of the guided tour, you will possibly find a tomb attendant who is more than willing to let you photograph inside the tomb for a price. Remember though to choose your moment carefully, when there are no other people around, and don't use the flash on your camera! (If nothing else, make sure you know how to turn off the automatic flash on your camera before travelling.)

Another important point is; always agree a price with the attendant before taking photographs otherwise he will demand an exorbitant amount of money and you may feel obliged to pay because he has done you a favour.

Although the above is a way around the photographic restrictions it is by no means satisfactory and we can only hope that the 'authorities' rethink their position on this matter.

Temple of Hatshepsut (Deir El Bahri)

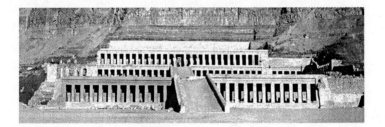

From the Valley of the Kings, you will probably be driven a short distance to the Temple of Hatshepsut. Here the coach will drop you off some distance away and visitors make their way up a long tarmac road to reach this splendid temple, whilst trying to side step as many of the local tradesman as possible who are there everyday peddling their wares. If you prefer you can take a little tourist 'train' that runs up to the site.

The temple's uppermost tier has only been reopened to the public for approximately 18 months after many years of closure due to excavation and restoration. When I last visited there was still some restoration work in progress mainly in the form of repainting the wall scenes.

Tourists on the long, hot walk up to the Temple of Hatshepsut

Temperatures at the temple can be very high with little chance of shade so take plenty of bottled water and a sun hat.

Valley of the Queens:

Next on the agenda could be the Valley of the Queens, where again three tombs are usually included. It should be noted that on my last visit there were only three tombs open! (Not including the tomb of Queen Nefertari, wife of Ramses the Great)

Personally, I find the Valley of the Queens not particularly interesting and its title a little misleading as most of the people buried there are either nobles or princes, not queens!

It should be noted that the recently restored Nefertari tomb will probably NOT be included in your visit. At present this tomb has a limited number of tourist tickets available each day (around 200) and generally speaking tour operators do not want to get involved with Nefertari's tomb due to the restrictions. It can also be closed to the general public without prior warning.

Most of the tomb areas and temples in Egypt cost only LE12 to visit but Nefertari's tomb, at the time of writing, will set you back 100 Egyptian pounds (£10). *One little note - all students get a 50% discount on production of a student card, or possibly some other means of identification.

It is very beautiful inside Nefertari's tomb and each wall is covered with bright, vivid paintings. However, in this particular instance, you really do have to carefully consider if it is worth the cost, especially as no photography is allowed. I will leave that decision up to you.

West Bank Tip 1: You will not be able to see all of the ancient sites the Necropolis has to offer on this one visit and what you will see will probably be governed by various factors including, tour company policy, guide, allotted time, popularity and possible site closure due to restoration or excavation work.

What I would therefore suggest is if you have some time to yourself during your cruise, (this usually happens in the afternoons, whilst moored at Luxor) then use it to make a return visit to the West Bank. You can easily hire a private taxi to take you to the places you missed on the first visit but ensure you agree a round trip price with him before leaving and stipulate that you want him to wait whilst you visit the sites. Also, make sure he is agreeing to a fee in Egyptian pounds, and not English!!

Alternatively, your holiday rep should be able to book a taxi for you at an agreed price. It may cost you a little more, but it will cut out the hassle of having to barter, especially if you are not comfortable with it.

West Bank Tip 2: I would also strongly recommend that you acquaint yourself with the West Bank sites before you visit, so you know exactly what you want to see. You can find a link to a list of recommended travel guide books at the end of this book. Or, for your convenience, you can use the link below:

http://www.ancientnile.co.uk/eb-links/travel.php

Other possible venues during your trip to the West Bank could be;

Medinet Habu - one of my favourite ancient sites at Luxor. You can see one of the smaller chapels (left) built by the female Pharaoh Hatshepsut.

Medinet is the Arabic named given to the huge Mortuary Temple of Ramses III. It is a magnificent complex containing two courtyards, Hypostyle Hall, sanctuaries, Palace ruins, small chapels, Nilometer, sacred lake, and mud brick enclosure walls.

Colossi of Memnon   Ramesseum

Seti Temple

Workers Village

Asasif and Noble Tombs

NOTE: For those of you travelling independently, the old kiosk where you used to be able to purchase tickets for all the different sites has now gone and you actually obtain them at each location. Unlike the photography ticket issue this, I believe, is an improvement!

An average time for a visit to the West Bank is four-five hours and on arrival back at the boat lunch will be ready to be served, after which the rest of the afternoon is usually spent relaxing on the sundeck. However if you are still in an explorative mood you could always take a trip into town. I tend to look around some of the hotels for future reference.

Getting Around Luxor

Depending on where your boat is moored you can either:

1. Walk into town. (If you feel up to running the gauntlet of the locals who are always on the look out for unsuspecting tourists. E.g. shopkeepers, taxi drivers, caleshe drivers, children etc.)

2. Take a taxi.

3. Use a traditional caleshe.

Caleshe: Horse and carriage transport

I remember once telling a particularly persistent caleshe driver that I wanted to walk, as it was healthier for me. But his quick retort was, 'Yes, but it wasn't healthy for him!' I had to laugh, and admiring his quick wit agreed to the ride. My advice is; try not to get too uptight with regards to the hassle, I'm afraid it comes with the territory.

Caleshe Tip: You may notice that some of the caleshe horses are in poor condition. Many have body sores, infected eyes or look emaciated. If you do decide to use a caleshe try to hire one who obviously looks after his horse and if possible tell the driver why you have chosen his particular carriage, then hopefully the conditions for the mistreated horses will improve.

Evening

After dinner you will probably spend the early part of the evening in the cruise lounge bar, or maybe attend the Sound and Light Show at Karnak Temple, which costs approximately £12 per person (US$20). Having been to three Light Shows, my order of preference are Giza (Cairo), Karnak and lastly Philae. I would recommend seeing at least one show, as I consider them to be quite unique.

Your tour company will probably have planned entertainment for the latter part of the evening, which could be anything from belly dancing to a local music band. And yes, the belly dancer will ask for volunteers, who are usually thin on the ground. Never keen on public humiliation, I tend to keep a low profile!

Day Two

Karnak and Luxor Temples

Whilst you are still moored up at Luxor your tour guide will probably arrange a combined trip to the two main temples in the city, Karnak and Luxor.

By far the largest of these is Karnak, which took over two thousand years to build and is dedicated to the ancient Egyptian god, Amun. The temple has the largest sacred lake in Egypt, where Pharaoh would ride his boat. This huge religious complex is my favourite ancient site. It is an incredibly imposing and wonderful place.

Compared to Karnak, Luxor Temple is much smaller and was dedicated to the Egyptian goddess Mut, Amun's wife. Outside the temple, two rows of sphinx statues line the road that originally led from Karnak to Luxor. Inside there are many huge statues of different Pharaohs and gods.

Karnak Temple entrance

In ancient time, during the Opet festival, which was usually held around the time of the inundation of the Nile, Amun's statue would be carried on a barge by the priests and taken from Karnak to Luxor Temple, where the god would be 'reunited' with his wife.

You can see in the Karnak photograph that there is a row of rams in front of the first pylon (large wall). These represent the god Amun to whom the temple is dedicated and it is known as Ram Road.

Karnak Temple and its sacred lake

Here Pharaoh's ritual boat would be ceremoniously rowed. In ancient times the lake had its own royal flock of geese.

Inside Luxor Temple

The inner courtyard contains huge statues of Pharaoh and the gods, which are very impressive.

Quite likely you will round this trip off with a visit to one of Luxor's papyrus galleries. Here you may be given a demonstration of how real papyrus is made and how not to fall victim to the 'banana-leaf' sellers. And just to make sure you don't, they will have a large collection of authentic papyrus for you to browse through and hopefully purchase.

Like the papyrus shop, other non-ancient trips during your cruise may include;

- Alabaster Factory
- Perfumery
- Nubian Village
- Bedouin Night
- Market /Bazaars
- Felucca ride
- Aswan Dam
- Mosque visit

Again the trip to the two temples will take about three to four hours, by which time you will probably be ready for your lunch.

If your cruise is following this common schedule so far, you are probably asking yourself, 'When are we actually going to set sail?' as by now you will have been on the boat for two days and not moved an inch!

But don't despair; chances are you will probably set sail that very afternoon, maybe even as you are eating your lunch. And at last you will actually feel as if you are on an Egyptian cruise. Even more so, as the industrial suburbs of Luxor finally give way to the wide open views of the river and countryside.

This is when you really get a feel for what life must have been like, as you can almost imagine yourself being transported back to a time when Pharaohs sailed the River Nile.

Egyptian village as seen from the cruise boat

At some stage during the evening, usually after dinner, the boat passes through the Esna locks and more often than not moors up in the town of Edfu.

Cruise boats passing through Esna Lock

Once again there will probably be some form of entertainment later in the evening. Quite commonly the captain will hold a small cocktail party where the management of the boat and your travel guides are introduced to everyone.

More often than not the cruise boats have to queue to get through the lock and this is the time when the local boatmen take the opportunity to surround the cruise ships and attempt to peddle their wares, day or night!

They do this by shouting to the people stood on the sundeck in order to get your attention. Once achieved, they then start to throw goods up onto the deck from some twenty feet below, mostly linen products; table cloths, towel, sheets, napkins, etc.

Items start going everywhere, on top of sun awnings, into the pool, on tables, chairs etc. And all the time these tradesmen will be bartering madly with anyone who will listen. Then, if a price is finally agreed the man will throw up a weighted pouch for the customer to put their money in.

This all sounds very friendly and a bit of fun, and for the most part it is. However this is not a game to these men, this is how they earn their living and they will attempt to get a sale anyway they can. (I will refer to Esna Lock and the boatmen again in the 'Telling You How It Is' section.)

Esna Lock Tip: It is worth bearing in mind that the Esna Lock is closed for routine maintenance at least twice a year – usually June and December. When this happens the cruise boats start their journey from Esna, rather than Luxor. If you intend travelling during these months I would definitely ask about this when booking, as Esna is approximately thirty minutes away from Luxor by coach. Therefore it is not easy to just take a trip into Luxor town. However, the upside is that prices for these cruises tend to be cheaper. My advice would be to ensure you check with your travel agent when the lock is closed before you book, so you won't be disappointed.

Day Three

Edfu Temple

Today you will probably visit the Temple at Edfu. Once again this is likely to involve an early start, something you are probably getting used to by now!

The magnificent Edfu Temple

Depending on numbers, this journey involves a five to ten minute drive in a horse-drawn caleshe, taxi, or privately hired mini bus. Edfu is a spectacular temple and one of the best-preserved ancient Egyptian sites.

Inside the courtyard at Edfu

Generally speaking your tour will last for approximately one hour at the end of which you may have a group photograph taken. One of the most popular spots for this is between the two large stone Horus statues in the main courtyard. The local photographer will deliver the photos to the boat later when you will have a chance to purchase a copy.

Visitors to the temple are given their guided tour outside and inside. To the right is the shrine, which would have housed the statue of the god.

This area was known as the inner sanctum, which in ancient times was only accessible to Pharaoh and the highest-ranking priests. Here the sacred statue of the god would reside to whom daily homage was given by way of food, chant and prayer.

Just outside of the temple there is a large local market where you may be given some time to explore and practise your bartering skills.

Edfu market. Where you may even pick up a few bargains!

But don't get too carried away as bartering can be a lengthy process and the tour group will not be too pleased at the delay.

If you are not interested in purchasing anything then it is best to avoid making eye contact with any trader and simply make your way back to your awaiting transport.

When you return to the boat, part of the afternoon will be spent relaxing on the sundeck whilst you set sail for Kom-Ombo, usually arriving mid-afternoon.

Depending on your schedule you may end up visiting Komombo soon after arrival, which involves a mid-afternoon tour. Luckily not many site visits take place during the hottest part of the day, but if this does happen at Komombo make sure you wear plenty of sun cream. Also carry plenty of bottled water as the heat can become quite overbearing and you will soon become dehydrated.

Kom Ombo Temple

Komombo temple is actually the only site still situated on the bank of the Nile and it was here that the crocodile god Sobek was worshipped. There are even a couple of mummified crocodiles on display.

After the tour ends, you will probably be left to make your own way back to the boat, which will be moored up only a short walking distance away.

Views of Komombo Temple

Bartering Tip 1: Again there is a local market just outside the Komombo temple, but as the temple actually overlooks the stalls you can check it out from a distance without the hassle.

View of the market from the Temple Walls of Komombo

However, I'm afraid there is still no escape from the hawkers who will still accost you as you make your way back along the quayside. Having said that I actually purchased a fine white cotton shawl for a very reasonable price from one of the traders.

Bartering Tip 2: As the men continue to try and sell you their goods just remember to keep walking as the price is likely to drop the closer you get to your boat, and the more desperate they are to make a sale before you are out of reach. Special Note: If you handle the goods, i.e. put them on, open them up, then the sellers are more likely to pressurise you into making a purchase.

During dinner the boat will have probably set sail for Aswan, which is the furthest south the cruise ship will travel.

Quite often in the evening there is an 'Egyptian Night' on board the boat. This entertainment involves fancy dress where you will be encouraged to dress up in a galabeya (local Egyptian costume) for dinner and party games.

Traditional Egyptian costume that you can purchase for the 'party'

Fancy Dress Tip: I have included a tip about this in the general section under 'Entertainment'.

Day Four

Aswan

This will probably be the start of a two-day stay in Aswan, which is actually my favourite city in Egypt, not particularly for ancient sites, but for its outstanding scenic beauty.

Usually the first day will be spent travelling by coach to the High Dam, which controls the Nile and is a major source of hydroelectric power in Egypt. Your guide will warn you against taking photographs in this sensitive area.

View from the high dam at Aswan

Sometimes the visit to the dam is followed by a trip to the old granite quarries, where an unfinished 137-foot (43-meter) obelisk lies abandoned due to a crack. This happened in antiquity when stonemasons were working it some 3000 years ago. I hate to think what happened to the person(s) responsible!

Quite likely you will finish your day's outing at the Greco-Roman Philae temple dedicated to the goddess Isis. Once you disembark from your coach the temple is reached via a short boat ride.

This temple, like Abu Simbel, was dismantled stone by stone from its original position on Philae Island and reassembled on Algikia Island to save it from being submerged when the Aswan High dam was built in the 1960s.

Quite often children also get onto the ferryboats trying to sell cheap souvenirs to the tourists, such as beaded necklaces and arm bracelets. Some are quite pretty, but don't expect them to last.

Philae Temple, which was dedicated to the goddess Isis and right, a traditional Nile boat known as a felucca

On your return to the cruise boat the tour representative may have arranged a felucca ride for you and your fellow companions to Kitcheners Island and its botanical gardens, or maybe just a scenic sail up and down the Nile. A felucca is a lovely, romantic and relaxing way to travel the river. Sometimes, if it's during the children's school break, you will find young boys paddling up to the feluccas in homemade canoes and asking for money or pens.

I usually photograph the children for 1 Egyptian pound each

In the evening there will probably be an opportunity for you to revisit Philae Temple for the Sound and Light Show, which costs approximately £12. You watch the first part of the show in different parts of the temple, including the main courtyard. Then you are taken to seats in the auditorium for the remainder. It was quite enjoyable but I think the latter half goes on a little too long.

As you are now in the old Nubian region of Ancient Egypt the evening boat entertainment could be authentic Nubian dancers or musicians.

Boats moored up at Aswan

Tombs of the Nobles at Aswan where ancient royals, officials and priests are buried.

Day Five

This day will either be spent at your own leisure, i.e., sightseeing, sunbathing or shopping. Or you may have opted for an optional excursion, the most popular being a trip to the Temples at Abu Simbel.

Other places of interest include Kitcheners, Kalabsha and Elephantine Islands; the Nubian Museum; the Old Cataract Hotel (one of Egypt's most famous and historic hotels); the Tombs of the Nobles and the Palace of Culture, where the artists perform Nubian stick dancing and sing folk songs about their village life.

Abu Simbel

Built by Pharaoh Ramses II around 1250 BC he dedicated one to himself and the other to his wife, Nefertari. His temple's most impressive feature is the facade where four giant colossi statues sit, each 65 feet (20 metres) high.

The temples at Abu Simbel, Ramses (left) Nefertari (right)

As with Philae, the Abu Simbel temples were dismantled in the 1960's from the original site to prevent them being submerged under the waters of the Aswan High dam. This was one of the greatest engineering feats of modern times.

You may, depending on your travel company, have a choice of either travelling by coach (approx. £70), or by plane (approx. £150) to Ramses' magnificent site. There may also be a daily hydrofoil to Abu Simbel, which costs approximately £50 (US$90). This price includes the return trip, meals, temple admission and a guide.

There is at least one police escorted coach convoy each day The trip takes roughly three-hours travelling through the desert and usually involves stopping to photograph the sunrise. On the return journey you may get the chance to take a camel ride.

Desert sunrise   Camel and handler

If you are travelling on one of the larger coaches then there may be a small coach toilet on board, which to be honest, is probably best avoided if at all possible. It is definitely not a trip I would recommend if you were suffering from 'Tut's-trots' or 'Pharaoh's Curse', common names for Egyptian stomach bugs.

Those taking the coach are usually woken around 3.30 am, and taken to the coach convoy assembly point for 4.00 am. The convoy usually consists of 30-40 coaches and once they start the journey they do not hang around. In the past there have been attacks on the desert road but since the police started escorting the coaches their presence has deterred further trouble. Before leaving you will have been issued with a packed breakfast, which you can enjoy on the journey.

By comparison the plane trip will take approximately 30 minutes but this is subject to cancellation if there are not enough numbers.

A panoramic view of Abu Simbel and the two temples
Ramses to the left, Nefertari on the right

These temples are unique because they were carved into the rock as opposed to being built stone by stone. The internal concrete and steel dome that helps to support the temple's structure can be visited via a small entrance to the right of the huge Ramses colossi.

Other optional excursion whilst you are in Aswan could be a visit to a Nubian Village via camel or boat, which cost approximately LE150 (£15) or a Bedouin Style dinner held in the desert at night.

You may also find that some of your fellow companions leave the ship at this stage and travel back to Luxor by coach. The reason for this is usually because they have booked a week in a hotel at Luxor (or maybe Aswan) and for them the cruise part of their holiday is over. You have to realise that the distance which has taken you three days to travel by boat, will in fact only take the coach four to five hours. (Approximately 125 miles /200-kilometer back to Luxor)

If this happens the advantages are; more room at the tables, less people on the sundeck and less time waiting for your drinks! However there will probably be no entertainment on board that evening as numbers are small.

Day Six

All day is spent sailing leisurely back downstream to Luxor as the Nile's blue waters gently flow by. This gives you time to unwind and chill out by the pool, or simply watch the world go by much as it did in ancient times.

The great river has sustained life in Egypt for the past 12,000 years and you can't help but marvel at its greatness as you cruise Pharaohs' Highway.

By this time your travel rep will have already advised you on the recommended amount of gratuities you should give the crewmembers, which will be divided amongst them at the end of the voyage. At the time of writing this was approximately £3.50 per person, per day. So for two people the total cost would be £50 GBP (US$90/Euro73). You will probably be asked to put the money into a sealed envelope before handing it into reception. The staff will then ask for your cabin number in order to record who has paid. It will also be suggested that you give your Egyptian guide a personal tip of about £25.

All these tips, which you are rarely told about when you book your holiday, can come to a considerable amount (not to mention a nasty surprise) and you will need to budget accordingly. You are never told that it is compulsory to provide these extra monies, however the method of request does make it hard to refuse.

You will probably reach Luxor early evening and as you prepare to leave the boat you may find the young men, who cleaned your cabins during the voyage, line up along the corridor in their best uniform, usually to the sound of a whistle. Whether you wish to give them an extra tip (which is basically what they are after) is entirely up to you.

However I would definitely tip the baggage handlers who carry your heavy suitcases (even two at a time) up very steep steps to the awaiting coach, which is no mean feat!

Day Seven

At the end of the cruise some package holidays may include a one or two day stay in a Luxor hotel before you fly back home. This option gives you a chance to either explore the town and sites on your own, or just chill out around the swimming pool and recuperate after the hectic itinerary.

Line of cruise boats moored up four deep at Luxor

Balloon landing after a trip over the West Bank at Luxor - as seen from the cruise boat

Boat Facilities

Any average size boat will have approximately 20-30 mainly twin-bedded cabins on two decks with WC, shower and air conditioning. There are usually a couple of larger suites with double bed, sofa bed and maybe a small bathtub. Some tour companies offer their guests guided tours of the boat during their stay on board, which may include the bridge, engine room and kitchen.

Generally speaking the main deck cabins have a slightly better view, as they are further elevated above the waterline. Also the lower deck can smell strongly of diesel, as they are closer to the engines, however the air conditioning usually defeats this - as long as you do not turn it off! The lower deck is also where you generally find the crew quarters situated. Cabin prices depend largely on which deck you sign up for, with the lower deck usually being the cheapest. If possible check out the plan of the boat before you book.

You will find that you are provided with blankets and will probably make use of them as the air-conditioning can make it feel pretty cold during the night. Of course you could turn it off, but depending on the month you are travelling, it could get very hot and sticky.

Rooms are cleaned daily by the young men employees, and in my experience, very well. You may find that your cabin boys are quite artistic and will leave you little surprises each day such as a pretty swan, crocodile, camel, boat and others, all made from the towels they leave in your room.

You will probably find a notice on the bathroom door about not putting paper down the toilet. If this is this case a separate bin will be provided for the soiled toilet paper. Be careful about adhering to this instruction as paper will inevitably block the toilet and cause a mess. The bins will be emptied every day.

You will find that the vast majority of boats have an all male Egyptian crew, with the one exception usually being your travel representative.

Facilities such as balcony cabins, cable television and library can vary from boat to boat so ask your travel agent for more details when booking. Usually the TV is pretty much a waste of time as most programmes are in Egyptian. If you are lucky you may get the US News channel NBC.

The average boat facilities include;

- ➢ Reception with seated area
- ➢ Restaurant
- ➢ Gift and jewellery shops
- ➢ Lounge bar and dance floor
- ➢ Sundeck with pool and canopied area

Splash pool and sundeck area

Typical canopied sundeck area on a Nile cruise boat

The lounge bar is the perfect place to relax on comfortable sofas and enjoy a drink before dinner. It is also the place, where the evening entertainment takes place, which can be anything from a disco to a belly dancing night.

The reception area usually has safety deposit boxes, whilst the shop(s) offer jewellery, souvenirs, clothing etc.

During the voyage you will probably have a chance to buy tee shirts with your name printed in hieroglyphs. In my experience they make novelty gifts for back home, but the quality is not very good and they tend to easily stretch out of shape, so I would only gently hand-wash them and preferably dry flat.

Gold is another very popular purchase; especially the cartouche necklaces, which have your name inscribed with hieroglyphs. Compared to UK prices the cost of gold is very good.

The photo shows some of the most popular ancient Egyptian designs namely; Eye of Horus (top left), Cartouche (top right), Ankh (bottom left), Scarab (bottom right)

However be careful where you purchase if you want to ensure value for money. The shop on the boat (and hotel shops) will give you a certificate that guarantees quality.

If you do decide you would like a cartouche necklace from the cruise jeweller be sure to order well before you are due to leave as orders can take a few days to make up.

Sundeck

On the sundeck you can relax and sunbathe, take a dip in the pool, watch the sites of the Nile pass you by, or just chill out under a sunshade with a book and cold drink. The large sundeck with the main amenities, including loungers, towels, and seated canopied area, is situated at the rear of the boat, whilst a smaller one can usually be found at the front of the boat, directly above the pilot's cabin.

Typical mosque as seen from the sundeck and pool area

Sun Deck Tips:

1. Be aware if you are sunbathing at the front of the boat near the steps that lead down to the pilot's area, you may be asked to join him by one of the boat's 'lower deck' crew. These are the manual workers; usually dressed in overalls, as opposed to the white shirt and black trousers worn by the waiters, guides, shop keepers etc. These manual workers are not normally seen in the tourist areas of the boat, but if you are close enough to the steps they may pop their head up and beckon you to come down.

Choosing whether to go or not is entirely up to you, but if you are a woman I would suggest that you do not go alone. Not that you are in any particular danger, but you will feel more comfortable with a friend around. They will probably ask if you want to toot the horn, or hold the steering wheel (whilst sat on the pilot's knee if he can get away with it) and will probably suggest that they take your photograph with the pilot if you have your camera with you.

As is usually the case, they do have an ulterior motive for inviting you down and that is - money. They will expect a tip for having 'shown you around', so if you don't want to be bothered, just shake you head and indicate you are not interested with a dismissive wave of the hand.

2. Sun shades (umbrellas) can be in short supply on the boat so grab one at the start of your sunbathing session, otherwise, when you've had enough sun, you may not be able to find one.

3. The pools onboard Nile cruise boats are not swimming pools but dip pools, so don't expect to be able to take a daily swim!

4. Occasionally the wind at the back of the sundeck swirls around and if you are not careful belongings can be snatched away overboard - e.g. sunhats, magazines, etc. However all is not necessarily lost, as you may be surprised when you look overboard and find one of the manual crew below has your lost item in hand. This is because the bottom deck acts like a funnel and drags most things back towards the boat where they are working. It is normal practice to thank the men with a suitable tip - after all they have rescued your precious belongings.

Meals:
Meals are served in the restaurant. You will find international and European-style cuisine widely available. Authentic dishes prepared for tourists are likely to be less spicy than found in the local restaurants. Breakfast is usually buffet style and spread over a couple of hours, with your choice of fruit juices, tea and coffee, cereal, rolls and

breads, cheese and meats, pastries, boiled eggs or omelette cooked to order. The wide choice means that vegetarians need not worry, as there are many vegetarian dishes available.

Lunch and dinner tend to be taken in one sitting, with a mixture of both waiter service and buffet style, with a wide selection of salad starters, delicious soup with fresh rolls and bread. During the cruise you will probably be offered a number of main course choices, including chicken, beef and fish dishes, fresh vegetables, pasta and rice. Desserts are numerous and you can often take your pick from superb pastries, creamy puddings, sponges, or gateau. Fresh fruit is also widely available and can include oranges, bananas, melon and fresh dates. On many cruises afternoon tea and cake is usually served on the sundeck whilst the boat is sailing.

If one night you decide to visit a local restaurant at one of the ports of call you might like to try some of the local delicacies:

- ❖ TAHINI: Sesame seed paste, mixed with garlic, spices and some olive oil, and served as a dip with bread.
- ❖ BABA GHANNOUGH: A dip made from tahini and mashed aubergines.
- ❖ FALAFEL: (also known as ta'amia.) Made from chickpeas pureed with garlic, fava beans, onions, egg and spices. A snack, which is freshly cooked and usually stuffed into pita bread with tomatoes lettuce and sauce.
- ❖ STUFFED VINE LEAVES: Minced meat and rice wrapped in vine leaves.

Drinks:
Meals are often accompanied by a range of drinks; choose from beer, coffee, wine, soft drinks, fruit juices, or just plain bottled water. Generally speaking Egyptian beverages are enjoyed without milk and with plenty of sugar, so if you require milk, be sure to ask for it, as it may not be offered automatically. (This is particularly the case if you eat out at a local restaurant.)

As a Muslim country the production of alcohol is restricted and the choice of beer is somewhat limited. The local beer is quite good, but not cheap at approximately £2 (US$3.60) a bottle. There are imported beers available such as Heineken but these are even more expensive.

Regarding coffee, unless you want Turkish style coffee, ask for a Nescafe. Some of the boats have coffee machines so it is possible to order cappuccino, espressos, etc. Away from the boat, tea is usually served in a glass, without milk and quite often flavoured with mint.

A variety of spirits and wines are readily available, though once again, expensive. The quality of local wines is improving but may not yet be up to the standards you are familiar with in the UK or the US.

Karkade is a local drink made from hibiscus petals; it's a rich burgundy colour and very thirst-quenching. It can be served either hot or cold. If it's not already sweet enough for you try mixing it with fizzy lemonade for a delicious long, cool drink.

Freshly squeezed juices such as orange and mango are widely available, with the local speciality being sugar cane juice.

Drinks Tip:

1. The general rule regarding drinks is that you do not pay when you order but settle the bill at the end of the cruise. You will be asked to sign for the drinks each time you order so make sure you keep the receipts for two reasons:

    a) You can keep an eye on the running total. It can come as a bit of a shock to find you have run up a bill of £200 on drinks without even noticing. As Egypt is mainly a Muslim country bare in mind that beer is very expensive and in many ways you are a captive audience!
    b) You can verify that your bill has been correctly totalled.

2. As mentioned previously, it is important to remember to drink plenty of water while in Egypt, particularly during the summer months; even if you don't feel thirsty, to prevent dehydration and stomach upsets.

4. Whilst on the boat you may come across some dodgy bartenders who, instead of signing and providing you with a drinks slip each time they serve you (as mentioned above), provide you with free drinks instead, but in return they expect you will give them money at the end of the cruise. They don't do it with everyone, but tend to target a few couples and give them the old tale of having too many wives and children to support. Whether you take them up on this 'offer' is entirely up to you.

Entertainment:

In general guest entertainment is provided in the lounge bar on most evenings. Usual treats can include a belly dancer, Nubian dancers, bands, disco or Whirling Dervish.

The lounge bar and dance floor area is where a belly dancer from the local town comes onboard to entertain the passengers in the evening.

The fancy dress Galabeya Party (Egyptian Night) is another very popular entertainment. This is where the tourists dress up in traditional Egyptian costume and join in party games led by your travel rep, with prizes for the winners.

Part of the activity may be to get divided into teams and take part in a Treasure Hunt Egyptian-style, and have fun searching the boat for unusual items on your list. Generally speaking there is no pressure to join in and if you prefer you can always retire to the sundeck for peace and quiet on a beautiful balmy evening and just listen to the waters of the Nile drift slowly by.

Music and a disco is also available on most evenings, although in my experience this is not widely taken up as many of the tourists retire to bed quite early as most mornings usually involve an early start, anything from 4am – 6am.

Entertainment Tips:

1. You will probably be encouraged to buy your Egyptian costume from the boat's shop by your Tour Rep, however you could find it a lot cheaper to purchase this from one of the local markets that you will undoubtedly visit before the Egyptian Evening. This does involve bartering though, so if it's not something you are comfortable with, stick to the onboard shop where your outfit will set you back about 100 Egyptian pounds.

2. Your photograph will be taken during the Egyptian Evening. You may be surprised to find the boat's photographer is also the shopkeeper, barber, and may also be available to do your pharaonic make-up for the evening!

Telling You How It Is

Now for the promise which I gave at the beginning of this book, about telling you 'how it is' and not over romanticising the holiday. From my experience the three main reasons most people are put off from going, or returning to Egypt are; Illness, Terrorism and Hassle.

Regarding Illness

Stomach Upsets: I'm afraid there are no readily available scientific statistics I can offer regarding how many people fall ill whilst in Egypt, only my own experiences, which are;

During my last eight visits to Egypt I have become ill twice, and both involved stomach upsets due to contaminated food. So in my case the chances were 25% in favour of becoming ill. The first was in 1996 when the most I had was diarrhoea, which I quickly had under control. The second was in 2003, when I contracted food poisoning and suffered with gastroenteritis (diarrhoea, stomach cramps, sickness, headaches). After a visit to the chemist and using my own painkillers, I was up and about again within thirty-six hours. At the end of the day there are no guarantees, so it's simply a case of weighing up how much you want to visit Egypt, compared to the chances of you becoming ill. And no matter what precautions you take, there are no guarantees.

Other causes of illness can be; change of diet, sunstroke, dehydration, alcohol overindulgence and even something as simple as coming back from a sightseeing tour taken in the scorching heat and going straight to your air-conditioned cabin. It is far better to first sit in the cooler (but not cold) boat lobby were you can acclimatise before returning to your cabin. Once there I would advise you to turn the air-conditioning off for a short while.

Malaria tablets: At present these are unnecessary, unless you intend travelling into the more remote areas of Egypt and in fact malaria tablets have many side effects including sickness and diarrhoea. However mosquito repellents are another matter and I would strongly advise you to pack these in order to minimize the chance of being bitten. Mosquito bites can be very annoying. If you are bitten use an appropriate antiseptic cream and try to avoid scratching the infected area as much as possible as the lump will just become itchier! I find gently stroking the lump with my fingertips or pressing just around the edges causes less irritation and helps to alleviate the overwhelming urge to scratch. A cold compress can also work wonders.

Regarding Terrorism

Egypt's tourism industry was crippled after the November 1997 attack by Islamic fundamentalist that left fifty eight foreign tourists and four Egyptians dead in Luxor at Hatshepsut's Temple. Although Egypt's key industry did begin to recover from the above incident, it was again hit by the troubles in Iraq.

There were three terrorist attacks on the 7th October 2004 at Taba and Nuweiba when 34 people were killed (including tourists) and 159 injured.

On the 7th April 2005 near the Khan El Khalili bazaar, 3 tourists were killed and 19 people injured.

Followed by another two attacks on tourists in Cairo at the end of April 2005 when 3 foreigners and 7 people were injured.

On 23rd July 2005 a number of bombs exploded in the vibrant resort town Sharm el-Sheikh when more than 200 people were injured and 83 killed from at least 5 different countries.

April 24th 2006 three bombs exploded in the bustling Egyptian Sinai seaside resort of Dahab, killing 23 and wounding 62 people.

Visitors should be aware that there is a high threat of terrorism in Egypt and I'm afraid no one can issue any guarantees of safety in this volatile part of the world. Attacks can be indiscriminate and against civilian targets, including holiday resorts. In order to help you make an informed decision I have included a few links at the end of this book.

However I will say this; If you are of a nervous disposition and are constantly worried by 'what may happen to you', then you really need to consider if Egypt is the ideal holiday destination for you, as such concerns will probably ruin your holiday.

Of all the Arab countries Egypt is considered to be one of the safest with crime and acts of violence being quite rare, especially in the tourist areas. After all, without the tourists many Egyptian livelihoods would suffer greatly. But as I stated above, there are no guarantees, so it would be wise to check out your government's foreign policy with regards to travelling to Egypt and the Middle East.

Egypt's police and security forces are making considerable effort to ensure the safety and security of foreign visitors by increasing security and they now insist on escorting travellers to remote areas. The risk of indiscriminate terrorist attacks against civilian targets, including places frequented by foreigners, means you should remain vigilant at all times and exercise caution in your daily activities – especially around crowded tourist areas such as Cairo.

The UK Foreign Office offers Security and General Tips to would-be travellers. (Worldwide - not just Egypt) You can find a link to this information at the end of this book.

Regarding Hassle

This can come in many forms such as:

- Pestering
- Tipping

- Bartering
- Scams
- Con Artists
- Intimidation (thankfully, not very common)

Pestering: In Egypt pestering can prove to be somewhat overwhelming, not to mention a little intimidating to the foreign traveller. And admittedly, at times, it can seem as if there are no genuine people in Egypt. Obviously this is not the case, but unfortunately, as a tourist you rarely come into contact with the more sincere people, but are constantly subjected to the ones who are only after your money. Therefore the benefits of a Nile cruise have to be noted.

- Firstly, the boat helps to shield you to against the constant pestering that people who are staying in hotels experience every time they walk out of the door. Also the majority of times you do venture off the boat you will be in the company of your fellow passengers, tour guide or rep and unlikely to be pestered.
- Another advantage is that, more often than not, your representative travels on the cruise with you, so they are readily available in cases of emergencies or simple advice, including hassle problems.

Tipping and Gifts: Away from the boat you will be expected to tip every time you are offered a service, have a meal, drink, etc. Tipping can really mount up, so make sure you have at least another £50-100 (US$90-180/Euro70-148) per person budgeted for this extra expense you are not always warned about. Otherwise you could find yourself running short of money. If someone does something for you in the tourist areas they are usually after a tip, e.g. ancient sites, airport, hotel. Don't feel obliged to pay every time, or you will soon run out of money!

You may have been advised by others who have travelled to Egypt to take things such as felt tip pens and sweets to give out as gifts to the local children.

I did this the first time I visited Egypt but made the mistake of handing a couple of them out in the centre of Luxor. The next minute I had children coming out of the woodwork until I was completely surrounded by tugging and snatching hands all fighting to get hold of the few sweets I had.

In the end they were even fighting amongst themselves with more than a few turning on the tears and begging me to give them one. Their ages ranged from as little as four to fourteen, so you can imagine some of them were quite strong. I never thought I was in any danger but for a while it was decidedly uncomfortable. Eventually a passing man shouted something in Arabic and they let go and I was able to make my escape.

Since that incident I only give out gifts in more controlled circumstances; maybe thrown from the boat, or where I know the numbers are small; for example at the ancient sites. The adults also like the pens, plus the toiletries such as shampoo and soap that are made available in your cabin.

Tip: I suggest you remove the pens from their packaging and hand them out singly; otherwise you will have the children fighting over the whole packet!

Don't be surprised by what you may be asked for. My husband has been asked for the shirt off his back, whilst one woman asked me for my sandals and another my lipstick. Needless to say these requests were politely refused.

Bartering: In all bazaars and shops bartering is common practice and can be fun, if approached in the right frame of mind. Your guide will be able to give you information on the best way to barter and also provide guidance on what you should expect to pay for common souvenirs such as papyrus, galabeyas, gold jewellery, leather goods, perfume, and spices. If you play your cards right you can get some good deals on these items compared to prices back home.

However, don't spend all your holiday trying to beat the Egyptians down to the lowest possible price. I remember one holidaymaker asking how much I'd paid for my private taxi across to the Valley of the Kings and when I told him he seemed to gain great delight in telling me how he had managed to get one for 20 Egyptian pounds cheaper.

But, as I pointed out, maybe he had saved himself £2 but at least our driver was friendly and not disgruntled by having been browbeaten into accepting a lower price. You have to remember that 20 Egyptian pounds is a lot to an Egyptian. If you have agreed on what you think is a fair price don't start feeling aggrieved just because you heard someone else got a cheaper deal. It only leads to dissatisfaction and annoyance, which undoubtedly could spoil your whole holiday.

Bartering Tips and Tricks

1. If you are with a partner there is a little trick that you can use. In Egypt, men are seen as the dominant sex (hmmm, I will say no more on the subject) and as such are treated with more 'respect'. Therefore, if you see something you would like to buy make sure that it is the female in the partnership that asks about the price of the item. Then, once the seller quotes a price, she can turn to her male companion and say 'do you like it?' At which point he should look totally disapproving and say something along the lines of; 'Why on earth do you want to buy that!"

Even if the Egyptian doesn't understand English, (and by the way, far more understand than let on) the seller will at least know from your partner's expression that he is not impressed and the seller will now feel under a certain amount of pressure to lower the price if he wants to ensure a sale.

At this point the woman can now start bartering and the chances are, if you both continue to play the game well, you should end up with a decent price. (But don't overplay your hand, or try doing it at the next stall!)

2. Another way to get people off your back is to tell them you are going home tomorrow and you have no money left, emphasising it by pulling out your pockets (making sure of course that you have no money in them!) or giving an open handed gesture. Also slang words for 'no money' such as 'skint', 'broke' etc are widely understood. The traders usually take this in good humour and may even make a joke about it. I remember saying this to one particular seller who looked at me with such feigned sadness before grinning and offering me (the poor little English woman) his can of coke. I couldn't help but laugh, as we both knew exactly the game we were playing!

3. Along similar lines, you can say you have left most of your money in the hotel for safety reasons and have only got so much with you. This works best if you make sure you have your 'budget' for the item in a separate pocket and pull it out, maybe making a point of counting it, as if you are uncertain how much you actually have left to spend.

4. When shopping please note that smiling politely or making a joke does not always work in your favour, as the seller often takes this as encouragement to continue. If you are unhappy with the attention the best course of action is to remain polite, disinterested and walk away. Be warned, if you look even the slightest bit undecided on an item, you will continue to be targeted. Once you get into the swing of things hopefully you will become more comfortable with the way things work and won't feel as pressured and start relaxing around the locals.

5. Sometimes felt tip pens can also be used as bartering tools. Many shopkeepers have young children and if you have nearly reached a price for an item, but he is still hanging back, offer to throw in a couple of felt tip pens and it may just clinch the deal for you.

6. Also try learning some basic Arabic phrases that will make sure you are clearly understood.

For example

ana bas bakhod felcra - I'm just looking

bikaam da - - How much is this

da ghaeli 'awi - It's too expensive

la' da kiteer 'awi - That's still too much

aekhir kalaem - Is this your best price

hashteree - I'll take it

hafakkar showaya - I'll think about it

bas keda shukran - nothing more, thank you

You can hear some of the above phrases spoken on our website at http://www.ancientnile.co.uk/eb-links/words.php

7. When you leave the boat on your own taxi drivers will accost you. Whenever this happens do not be afraid to ask who is the cheapest. This can cause some animated scenes though, as they will argue vigorously amongst themselves whilst you stand there waiting. Then, if you find a taxi driver, guide, etc whom you particularly like then get his name and ask for him personally.

8. Not so much a tip but a suggestion. Bartering is a matter of attitude and in order to 'survive' you have to approach it as a challenge and not an ordeal! Simply learn from your encounters (and mistakes) and above all don't let it spoil your holiday. If you feel your temper rising - walk away.

Scams: You will find children of all ages trying to sell you something, be it jewellery, papyrus bookmarks, little ceramic ornaments, plastic pyramids etc. On occasion some will give you an item for you to inspect and then refuse to take it back. In this instance, if you do not want to purchase the item, simply put it down on the ground and walk away.

Adults do not tend to work in this way, but be wary of those asking if you would like them to take your picture. It has been known for them to refuse to give back your camera unless you give them money.

You will often have to run the gauntlet of traders at many of the ancient sites and towns. If they try to give you a 'free' gift do not accept, as this is merely a ploy to get you to buy something. It's best to politely refuse and carry on walking. Keep in mind, that vendors do not give something for nothing, whether in Egypt or England.

Con Artists: They are about and use various methods to get you to part with your money. Besides the above tricks, you should also watch out for;

• Children who turn on the crocodile tears.

• People who demand extra money because you paid up front. (E.g. it has been known for camel riders to ask for more money to complete the return part of your journey)

• People selling imitation goods. Such as papyrus made from banana leaves that break up within days. You can test if they are genuine by asking if you can roll them up before buying – if they split they are made out of banana leaves. Or cheap leather shoes / sandals made from camel rather than cowhide. Even saffron can be fake. You may see a huge bag at a very cheap price but unless you know what saffron looks like take care. Saffron should be fairly long strands about a centimetre long and coloured a deep orangey red. The strands should not be short and powdery. (I won't go into what it may be made from!)

- Local tradesmen in the bazaars who will tell you that they work part-time on your boat, pretending to know you and asking why you don't recognise them. This is purely to make you feel guilty enough that you will buy something from their shop. They may even have a photograph of a boat that looks just like yours. I suggest you call their bluff by asking them the name of the boat you are travelling on. I bet they don't come up with the right answer! (By the way - if by sheer luck they do guess correctly, tell them they are mistaken.)

- Watch out for the ones who also stop you on the street, asking, 'Do you remember me?' or 'Don't you remember talking to me yesterday?' Usually taken by surprise most people say, 'Yes, I think so...' And then before they know it they are being frogmarched by the elbow into a shop for the hard sell.

- Local men who approach foreign men asking if they want a 'good time'. Usually this scam is set up in order to rob you. Do not go with anyone who comes up to you on the street, the same way, as you wouldn't just go off with a stranger if you were approached in the UK. Keep safe. Remember Egypt is a Muslim country with strict sexual laws.

- Locals who say that a particular road is closed, or they know a quicker route and then take you via a bazaar where the shopkeeper pays them commission.

- When paying for anything, including carriage rides or taxi fares, make sure you point out the money you are giving them. For example if you are paying with a LE50, say so out loud as you hand the money over to them so they can not quickly switch the note for a similar looking 50 piastres note. This is a really common scam, which if they get away with it, can leave you LE495 out of pocket. Similarly if you are handing out several notes, count them out loud as you put them into their hand. If they still try it on, and you are confident that you gave them the correct money, hold your ground and let them know you are not pleased that they are trying to take you for a ride This will usually shame most of them into backing down. Do not become distracted by others, especially when dealing with large amounts.

- Beware of drivers that work in teams. Quite often a few may play the part of harassers, whilst one will act as the rescuer – seemingly coming to your aid by seeing the others off and thereby gaining your trust.

- Watch out for those drivers who suggest you visit their homes. Usually they want to make you feel sorry for the conditions they live in so you will give them money or gifts. You may well also be told a sob story about how one of the family is at death's door and in need of urgent medical treatment.

- Shopkeepers sometimes strike up friendly conversation during a sale hoping you will not notice that they have short-changed you.

- Watch out for the unofficial bottled water sellers who have simply collected empty bottles and filled them for the domestic supply. This can easily be avoided by checking to see that the seal is intact around the cap.

- Take care with people would who take advantage of your lack of local knowledge.

This happened to us during our first trip to Cairo. After being dropped off by a taxi we were looking at a map to find the location of the antiquities museum when an Egyptian came up to us and asked if we needed assistance. We told him it was okay as we realised the museum was just round the corner. However, as he spoke excellent English, he started to strike up a friendly conversation, asking us where we were from, and how his wife was English and now taught in Cairo. I have to admit it was a very polished act and we were taken in hook, line and sinker.

Then, when we were just about to take our leave he mentioned that the museum didn't actually open for another hour and if we wanted he had a shop not far away where we were more than welcome to pass the time. Uncertain, but not wanting to appear rude, we agreed, especially as he assured us he was not after any sale.

Well, as you can imagine once we were in the shop we were presented with a couple of free cokes (a common practice), followed immediately by the hard sell! In the end, due to our naivety we spent about £50 on a papyrus and when we eventually returned to the museum it was to find it had been open all the time. So beware 'good Samaritans' - or Egyptians with gift shops!!

It has to be said that scams and intimidation are more prevalent in Cairo than Luxor.

The infamous papyrus!

Intimidation: This is by far the worst type of hassle and deserves no tolerance. Fortunately though, it is not a particularly common problem.

Again, I'm sorry to say that women are the most vulnerable and may be approached even within the Ancient sites. Above all, if approached do not give in to their demands for money, and tell them you will call the police (*bolees*) if they do not leave you alone.

Unescorted women can also be subjected to sexual harassment and verbal abuse, particularly young girls who may also be hassled by the local male youths. Arab women are generally helpful and will usually respond to a female in distress.

If you decide to do some sightseeing on your own, be aware of the men who say they must show you around the ancient site – that is not true. Tell them straight that you are looking around the site on your own.

It has also been known for some men to force their way into taxis around the various sites demanding to act as guides. If this happens refuse to be intimidated and decline their offer point blank. If he then refuses to leave, get your taxi driver to evict him. You will probably find that he will do this quite willingly, as he will be worried that you will not pay him!

I mentioned earlier about passing through the Esna locks and it was here on my first Nile cruise that I encountered intimidation for the first time. It was already dark when we reached the locks and like many others I had decided to go up onto the deck to watch whilst people bartered with the vendors.

Just a short distance away, a woman who was similarly dressed, had been trying to agree a price for a tablecloth which one of the boatmen had thrown up to her. However, when things got a little heated the woman suddenly walked away when the boatman wasn't looking and unfortunately he then mistakenly started shouting the odds at me, saying I had stolen his goods and that he was going to inform the police. At first I tried reasoning with him calmly but in the end I had to walk away due to his aggressive and threatening behaviour. Needless to say I was very annoyed and more than glad to see the back of the lock as I kept expecting the police to board at any time.

One final note on this matter; I didn't tell this story in order to stop you buying from the boatmen, as I'm sure most of the encounters pass off without incident. By recalling this event I merely wish to make you aware that sometimes things can get a little out of hand, especially as this is a fairly unique situation where the vendor is some twenty feet below you and at a distinct disadvantage. As you will discover during further encounters, this disadvantage is a rare situation.

If you experience any sort of intimidation in any situation immediately tell your travel representative or travel guide.

Below I have included some Arabic phrases you could memorise. You can hear some of them spoken on the following web page: http://www.ancientnile.co.uk/eb-links/words.php

sebni fi haelee - leave me alone

hatemshi walla a Tlobi bolees - Go away, or I'll call the police

fi wahid biyedaye'ni - there is someone bothering me

For recommended Arabic phrase books visit the following website link:

http://www.ancientnile.co.uk/eb-links/arabic.php

General Information

1. To fully enjoy your Egyptian cruise, it's important to choose an experienced company who operate some of the three hundred plus boats that sail between Luxor and Aswan. When choosing, look for a company who pride themselves on offering comfortable accommodation and first-class service. There are usually some very reasonably priced late-deals, which is great, if you don't have to book your holiday in advance.

2. For most westerners who prefer a more temperate climate the months of March, April, September, October, November, are usually good choices. It has to be said that there is also nothing wrong with travelling to Egypt during the months of December, January or February except with regards to temperature and daylight hours. These months are Egypt's winter season and as such can be on the cool side. I like to incorporate my holiday with time spent relaxing around the pool in comfortable temperatures. For example today in Luxor at 11.30am (January 5th) the temperature was 13C (55F) which is a little on the cool side for my tastes. Also because it's winter, there are less daylight hours available for sightseeing. Again this is a personal choice and depends entirely on what you require from your holiday. Egyptian summers on the other hand are scorching, especially in the South, (e.g. Aswan) but it means there are fewer crowds and cheaper prices – basically it depends on whether you can tolerate such temperatures? When I checked the real time temperatures in Luxor on the 15th July at noon it was 105 degrees – melt down time! For real-time temperatures go to:

   http://www.ancientnile.co.uk/eb-links/traveltemp.php

3. Ensure you get yourself a good Egyptian travel guide and phrase book and read up on the sites before you travel as this makes the tours far more interesting.

4. Packed lunches are provided if you are travelling during meal times - e.g. to Abu Simbel.

5. The extras, which will not be included in your holiday, are; tips, drinks tab, cruise photographs and additional excursions, so you will need to budget accordingly.

6. When visiting Egypt you should have a full, current passport valid for at least six months. You will also require a visa which can be obtained either before you leave, or on entry to the country (most popular method) at a cost of approximately £20.

7. The further south you travel the hotter it becomes. So Aswan can be several degrees hotter than Luxor and Luxor several degrees hotter than Cairo. Depending on the time of year, when you first step off the boat in the mornings it can feel as if the heat is literally scorching your lungs. This is due to the huge difference between the air conditioned boat and the heat outside. It will wear off, as you gradually become acclimatised.

8. Egypt is not a particularly popular holiday destination for young children. By this I mean, most children are not particularly interested in visiting 'ruins' every day. However teenagers who have studied Ancient Egypt can usually appreciate the 'wonders' and have a great holiday. The average age of those taking cruises I would say is 40 to 50 with only a few teenagers, however you will find that many of the adults on board will be more than happy to include the younger generation in their conversations. Many travel companies do not allow children under the age of twelve to travel on cruises.

9. Due to operational difficulties, Nile Cruise itineraries can be subject to alteration at short notice, especially during the closure of Esna Lock. During certain periods, you may find that the boat has to sail after dark, thereby reducing daylight sailing hours and scenic views.

10. When your boat moors up you may find that other vessels have to come alongside to dock and depending upon your cabin location your views may be restricted or blocked all together which will diminish the available light. This is a particular problem in the busy season.

11. There are no longer crocodiles in the Nile between Cairo and Aswan due to the building of the high dam.

12. The Nile cruise boats are flat-bottomed and as there is no tide, you will not get seasick.

13. In order to leave the boat you will be required to walk along a roped gangplank, and there may be quite a few high and steep steps to climb in order to reach the main road. You can see a demonstration of this in the mobility section.

14. If you are celebrating a special occasion, such as your wedding anniversary let your travel rep know and most likely you will be presented with a cake during dinner by members of the staff who will then probably sing and play tambourines. They will of course expect you to join in and maybe dance with them and then eat part of the cake together. (If you are of a reserved nature like myself - then best to keep mum!)

15. Departure Day – If your flight does not leave until evening you will probably be given two options. One, to vacate your cabins by early morning, or secondly, to pay an extra fee (usually around £15 per cabin) to keep the use of your cabin until about half an hour before you depart for the airport. Needless to say, nearly everyone chooses the second option.

General Medical and Safety:

a) It is important that you do not travel to Egypt without adequate medical insurance and make sure it

66

covers the costs of local hospitalisation and medical repatriation to your own country.

b) The majority of Nile cruise boats DO NOT have a ship's doctor.

c) Tell your travel rep if you become ill, as they are experienced in these matters. Also it's best if you have your illness recorded, in case you need to complain to your travel company at a later date.

d) I have to say hospital facilities in Luxor and Aswan are inadequate and they are almost non-existent at most other ports of call along the Nile. However many hotels have English speaking doctors on call 24 hours. Prices for doctors are difficult to give as each set their own fees, but expect to pay in the region of LE200 and about LE30 for a prescription.

e) Many prescription drugs are available over the counter in Egyptian pharmacies but they may be called by a different name and unless you know, it is best not to take any chances. So if you have prescribed medicines ensure that you take them with you.

f) As mentioned previously, stomach upsets can occur due to; Food poisoning, Excessive heat (Sunstroke), Change of diet, Dehydration. I would advise taking plenty of anti-diarrheic with you (e.g. Imodium), also painkillers that are gentle on the stomach, (e.g. Paracetamol) and a stomach remedy (e.g. Gaviston). However if you do forget, the local chemist will be able to help. Obviously sickness can greatly affect your enjoyment and ability to go on organised tours. Unfortunately there is no sure way of avoiding food poisoning, but you do have some control over the last three in the list; namely, avoid overdoing the sunbathing, wear plenty of sun cream and don a sunhat, take it easy with the food intake and don't overindulge in spicy foods, avoid excessive amounts of alcohol and drink plenty of bottled water. Having checked through many a hotel travel guide book in my time (including all the major tour operators) I find that most will try to persuade you that food poisoning is low down the list for causing stomach problems but I have to say, from my own personal experience, it is the highest. Obviously the tour operators do not want you to think hygiene is not of the highest standard in Egypt and would prefer you to be the cause of your own illness. If you are still ill after returning home, e.g. any stomach cramps, loose motions, diarrhoea, sickness, intestinal discomfort then visit your doctor as soon as possible. Most likely you will be asked to provide samples to determine the cause of the infection, which could be either bacterial or viral. And remember to inform your travel company about the poor hygiene standards. Unless they are aware of the situation then nothing will change.

g) Egypt can be a bit of a culture shock at first and do not expect that health and safety and medical care to be up to western standards. However standards in most of the hotels and cruises are good and provide a decent service.

h) Do not be tempted to swim in the Nile or canals as you are at GREAT risk of exposure to bacterial infections, hepatitis, and parasites.

Photograph showing dead camel floating in the Nile.

For the most part the Nile looks and smells clean and you will most likely see children frolicking in the shallows or swimming, and you may see adults washing in it - but do not be tempted to jump in yourselves.

i)   Also avoid walking barefoot for the same reasons as above, this includes inside the temples and pyramid sites. I often see 'Kemetics' (modern day followers of the Ancient Egyptian religion) meditating or wandering around the temples barefoot, especially Karnak, and I often wonder if they are aware of the risks.

j)   Whenever possible wash your hands after handling Egyptian money as this can be a source of infection – especially stomach upset.

k)   Drink only bottled water: 2 litres will cost anything between LE5-9 (50-90p). However you can use tap water to wash, bathe and clean your teeth.

l)   Generally speaking I would not recommend that people travel into the smaller villages unless you are with somebody you trust, who knows the area and language. This is especially true at night.

Disability, Special Needs and Mobility Problems

1. If you travel in the busy season you may have to walk through as many as eight boats across gangplanks to get on and off your own boat. Although the ones between the boats are usually quite substantial, the landing gangplank can be particularly narrow.

2. It has to be said that the condition of some of the disembarkation areas can be rough and rocky with very high steps you will need to climb in order to get onto the main road.

Steep steps (to the left) that lead up to the main road and a roped gangplank (to the right) that you will need to cross in order to get on and off the boat.

3. These riverside areas can also have obstacles such as mooring ropes, chains, tools etc; which can make them awkward to negotiate for those with walking difficulties.

4. Most of the ancient site visits involve early morning starts; which can create their own difficulties for the less mobile.

5. Some of the ancient sites are on rough terrain and many of the temple floors are uneven. Most tombs involve bending, steps and/or steep ramps.

It really does depend upon the degree of the infirmity as to how much help you will need and how well you will be able to cope. I would definitely discuss any mobility problem with your travel agent/tour company before booking and ask if they make any special arrangements for people with your particular needs.

General Photography

Some museums and historical sites may not allow the use of cameras and video equipment, while others may charge a fee, usually around LE5-LE10. While you may usually take pictures from the outside of most monuments, many demand that you do not use a flash when taking pictures inside, even if you have paid a photography fee. The use of video cameras and tripods can be even more restricted, and a larger, additional fee is often payable. Photography is strictly forbidden at military installations, public works and government buildings. Tourists should not take photographs that include official uniformed personnel.

Always ask permission before photographing local Egyptians, and expect to be asked for a tip in return. Around the sites you will often be approached by local men or boys, who will indicate that you should photograph them, again if you do, they will expect a tip. I always let them know before I take a picture, how much I am willing to pay, (e.g. 1 Egyptian pound), but remember that will 'buy' you one picture only, if you take more they will expect more. Plus, even if you only take one they will still try it on and ask for more, e.g. another pound for his horse, camel, ailing mother etc. Be firm and say, no. (La' a)

Photography Tips

I have heard it suggested that it is often best to wait until you get to Egypt to buy your film, as it's much cheaper than in the UK, and you can also barter for a discount if you buy two or more films. However, in my experience, although the film is cheaper, you cannot always be sure how the film has been stored and therefore the condition of the film. Also finding a place that actually stocks the film you want may be a chore in its self. Therefore I would still advocate taking a few rolls of film with you, especially if this is a-once-in-a-lifetime holiday. After all, you do not want ruin your chances of having some great photographs to look back on just for the sake of saving a few pounds.

If you use specialised film, e.g. slide, infrared, high or low ASA (ISO) ensure you take this with you, as searching for this type of film could be very time-consuming. Then, if you do happen to chance upon a shop that does sell your type of film, you can always buy some for use at home, or during the rest of your holiday.

I once bought a disposable waterproof camera from a shop only to find when I returned home that the camera had already been used and refilled with duff film. Needless to say, no photos turned out and I learnt my lesson.

I am not saying that all shops are unscrupulous but just be aware that it does happen. If you do decide to buy, check all packaging carefully to make sure nothing has already been opened. If required, there is more information in our 'Photographing the Ancient Sites' book, which is available from www.ancientnile.co.uk

Clothing and Accessories

It can be hot throughout the year in Egypt; especially during the day so loose fitting 100% light cotton clothing is the most comfortable and most sensible choice.

Take a good pair of sunglasses, comfortable walking shoes, or trainers, plenty of sun cream, swimwear and a good sunhat.

Women, in particularly, are best advised to dress conservatively. It is wise not to have bare shoulders or wear revealing tops or shorts in the towns and villages and especially when visiting mosques and churches as you could risk causing offence. Egypt is a Muslim country and Egyptians, particularly the older generation, do not appreciate seeing flesh on show.

Likewise, women showing too much skin can also provoke unwanted attention from the younger Arab men. This is particularly true with regards to skimpily clad young women. It is not my intention to be moralistic here, this information is provided because I wish to tell you how it is, and not what you, or I, think it should be like.

It is also not acceptable for men to go bare-chested except by the pool and women going topless is not allowed anywhere.

I find the best clothing to wear is loose cotton clothing because it allows your skin to breathe in the hot weather.

Casual dress is okay on a cruise and evenings are informal. Jacket and tie or cocktail dresses are not necessary, but I usually take a couple of dresses that are classed more as 'smart evening wear'. Plus, it's nice sometimes just to spend an hour or two getting yourself ready for the evening as it makes you feel as if you are on holiday.

The months in Egypt follow the same seasonal pattern as the UK, e.g. July is summer and January is winter but obviously Egypt's are a lot hotter and milder respectively, especially the further south you travel. As most of us choose to visit during the cooler seasons I would also suggest you take some warmer items of clothing just in case the temperatures drop, (especially in the evening) e.g. one light cardigan or jumper, trousers, light jacket etc. You can see an average temperature chart on the following web page:

http://www.ancientnile.co.uk/eb-links/travelinfo.php.

Plus, there is a real-time temperature page for most of the major Egyptian cities at

http://www.ancientnile.co.uk/eb-links/traveltemp.php

So, once you have booked, I would suggest you check out this page regularly during the few weeks before you travel to see what the weather is like. Clicking on any of the 'city temperature bars' on the website will take you to a more detailed page.

Local Customs

Quite often you will see Egyptian male friends greeting each other with a hug and kiss on both cheeks, but not friends of the opposite sex. You may also see, as you walk around the towns that many boys will hold hands. This is common practice.

As a foreigner, when you are introduced to someone, or when you are saying goodbye to someone you have got to know during your stay, (e.g. Egyptian guide) it is best to stick to a hand shake.

Showing open affection to your partner in public places is definitely frowned upon.

There is a definite class system in Egypt so don't be surprised if you see one man chastising another quite severely. I once witnessed a hotel manager slapping a poor pool attendant a number of times around the head. The 'lower class' must show respect and will bow to their 'superiors' at all times. Again, whether you agree, or not, this is the way of things in Egypt. As much as you may want to say something I would suggest you don't as you could cause the person even more trouble, once you take your leave.

Money Matters

The local currency is the Egyptian pound and at the time of writing the exchange rate was around 10 Egyptian pounds to £1 GBP. (E.g. 10p)

At the time of writing the maximum amount of Egyptian currency that can be taken into Egypt is 5,000 Egyptian pounds per person. However this is subject to change and you will be informed as to the current limit when you purchase your currency.

Notes are in denominations of LE 100, 50, 20, 10, 5 and 1. Some of the notes look very similar on first glance, so when buying souvenirs be absolutely sure which note you are handing over – 50 piastres, not 50 Egyptian pounds! I am sure you will be told of your mistake if it's a 50 piastres note, but not if it's LE50! That's equivalent to £5 GBP and a definite windfall for most Egyptians. The average hourly rate for a waiter is 1 Egyptian pound (10p).

In June 2006 two new coins are expected to be introduced that will replace the LE1 and 50 piastres notes that will eventually be withdrawn.

Examples of the smaller Egyptian notes (1,5,10)

Credit cards and travellers cheques are widely accepted but outside of the big cities their usage is extremely limited as Egypt is still largely a cash based country. American Express, Diners Club, MasterCard and Visa are all widely accepted. There are cash machines in the main towns and most of which now accept all the major cards. Whilst in Luxor a representative from the local bank usually visits the boat. (Your Travel Rep should advise you during your welcome meeting).

Banks will charge a small commission fee to change your currency or travellers cheques and will require you to present your passport. An official receipt will be given when exchanging money, which should be kept for inspection. To avoid additional exchange rate charges, travellers are advised to take travellers cheques in US Dollars, Euros or Pounds Sterling. Banking hours are normally Sun-Thurs 0830-1400.

Tipping, or baksheesh as it is called in Egypt, is a way of life and porters, ancient site attendants, waiters etc will all expect a small tip for their services. The average is about LE1 for a porter, and LE2 for a coach driver. However, on a Nile cruise, you may be asked to either pay a sum of money at the start of your cruise from which your guide will pay all off-boat tipping, or you may be expected to pay yourself as you go along.

Money Tips:

1. Hold on to small notes, LE1 and LE5 in particularly, as they are very useful for tipping and to buy cheaper items. Change always seems to be in short supply in Egypt, even the locals do not like to part with small notes!

2. If you end up with some of the small notes left over at the end of your holiday, you will probably find when you arrive at the airport that some of the local baggage carriers are eager to exchange them for English coins, which they have acquired from tourists who have just arrived. This is an ideal way of getting rid of them as fair exchange is no robbery, and everyone is happy. Of course this applies to any foreign currency - not just the English pound.

Miscellaneous:

o   The electricity supply is 220 volts, 50 cycles, so an adaptor is necessary (usually two-pronged)
o   The language is Egyptian Arabic, however English is widely spoken in the tourist areas.
o   Telephone calls are not usually available on the boats. I always take my mobile phone with me for emergencies - making sure that International calling is switched on. It is expensive to telephone home from hotels, however you can get phone cards, which cost LE20 or LE30 for an approximate 3-4 minute call to the UK. Again your travel rep will be invaluable as a source of local knowledge.
o   Most cruise boats have safety deposit boxes available for clients use and these are often provided at no extra charge.
o   Shops are generally open 10am to 9pm in winter and 9am to 10pm in summer, with many being closed on Sunday. In the tourist areas some shops may stay open outside these hours. Do not be surprised if you are offered tea or a soft drink in larger shops, as this is customary.

Travelling Alone

I am often asked if I would recommend travelling alone. This depends entirely upon the individual and how confident and comfortable you feel with the idea. If you have any doubts I would suggest travelling in a group, at least for the first time. It will also depend upon your gender; women on their own are likely to feel more uncomfortable than men.

For the above reasons I firmly believe a Nile cruise is particularly good if you are travelling alone as meal times are usually spent with the same people each time on tables that may seat anything from 6-12 persons.

The same can be said of the organised tours where the same group of people usually view the sites together. This allows you to meet and chat with others, (or not as the mood takes) so generally speaking you don't feel as isolated as you may in a hotel.

Getting Married in Egypt

I have been asked on occasion whether it is possible to get married during a Nile Cruise and the answer I'm afraid is, no.

It is possible to get married in Egypt, but it is not easy and you certainly can't get married around the ancient sites.

In order to get married you have to meet certain government requirements and time periods (if divorced or widowed) before you can get wed. Plus, a marriage in Egypt is only legal if it is a civil ceremony performed at a local marriage court. There could also be some doubt as to whether the marriage would be classed as legal in your own country of origin. (See links at the end of the book for further details). 'Orfi weddings' or secret marriages are not legal.

Summary

As I mentioned at the beginning, this book should be used as a general guide as every cruise will have its own itinerary, entertainment programme and food menu. What I have tried to do is give you the most popular sites and activities that you may come across, plus a few personal insights into the way things work.

Having read this book you may be thinking – is Egypt for me? The problem with writing a 'telling you how it is' book is that the negatives can appear to outweigh the positives. However, to put things into perspective I have to reiterate that in all probability the worst you will encounter on your holiday is pestering from the local Egyptians who work the tourist areas. Whilst this hassle is annoying, you just need to get used to saying, 'No thank you' (La'a shukran) without thinking you are giving offence. Also a cruise will 'cushion' you against most of the nuisance. Egypt is no worse than many of the other Arabic countries in this regard, for example Tunisia. Also the magnificent ancient sites, such as the temples and tombs, more than make up for any hassle you may encounter.

I firmly believe that Nile cruises are the best introduction to Egypt as they provide excellent value for money and access to sites that you may miss out on during a hotel based holiday. Plus, it is the most enjoyable way to view the country for the first time as you glide up and down the river from the comfort of your boat. I have heard it commented by some that a cruise may be 'too touristy for them' but in my opinion it is still the easiest way to get a feel for the country and the ways of the people, so hopefully by the end of your holiday you will know if you would like to return and visit other areas like Cairo and the pyramids.

I hope you have enjoyed reading this as a small flavour of what to expect during your Nile Cruise and as the saying goes, 'forewarned is forearmed'. ☺

The next section contains a list of the other books in this 'Travel Egypt' series, a link to our music CD that has been specially produced for the website ancientnile.co.uk and pages that contain information regarding Egyptian gods, symbols and historical facts. There is also a list of external links that direct you to many multimedia products including, holidays, travel guides, phrase books, Egyptian gifts, freebies and official government websites etc, which we hope you find useful. (All these Internet links were available at the time of publication.)

If you decide a Nile cruise is for you, then have a fantastic Egyptian holiday.

Egyptian Symbols

 Ankh: Believed to unlock the mysteries of heaven and earth. Hence, the reason it is referred to as, 'The Key of Life'. The design appears to combine the symbolic cross of Osiris and the oval of Isis. It is often shown being carried by the gods and pharaoh.

 Cartouche: Sign for Encircling Protection. In the form of a knotted rope it was used to enclose the royal name of the pharaoh. As with the Shen hieroglyph the cartouche signified the concept of surrounding protection. The cartouche may also have symbolised the universe being circled by the sun. Even the sarcophagi of some of the 18-19th dynasty pharaohs take on this shape and some tombs are also cartouche shaped, e.g. Tuthmoses III, affording the king that extra protection.

 Crook (Sceptre): Symbol of Guardianship. The symbolism of the crook is similar to that of the stick and its derivatives, namely, power and authority. The royal Egyptian symbol was called *'Heka'* when it was in the shape of a shepherd's crook and a *'Was'* when it had the head of a canine animal and a two-pronged base. The triple sceptre was made up of a whip, a staff and stick, representing domination over matter, control of feeling and domination of thought. It is a symbol of the central axis, like the king himself, the intermediary between god and his subjects, a guarantee of peace and justice. The royal symbol of the kings was adopted from the god Osiris and the ancient shepherd deity, Andjeti. It denoted Pharaoh's role as guardian of the People of the Nile. The crook and flail were used in all royal ceremonies and were part of the mortuary regalia of the kings, ensuring the continued welfare of the diseased in the Afterlife.

 Djed Pillar: The symbol of Osiris, god of the Dead. In the book of the dead it is described as Osiris' backbone. It seems to have come to represent stability. Other gods that have been associated with it are Sokar and Ptah. It was at Memphis that the ceremony known as, '*raising the djed pillar*' was probably first carried out by Pharaoh, which represented the stability of the monarchy and the resurrection of Osiris. The best depiction of this act is in the Osiris Hall at Abydos.

 Eye of Horus: Sign for Healing. During his confrontations with the god Seth, Horus is said to have lost his left eye, which represented the moon. However his wife, the goddess Hathor, restored it. That is why the *wedjat* (Eye of Horus) symbolises healing. Extremely common as an amulet it represented strength, protection, perfection, and the act of 'making whole'.

 Flail: A symbol of Guardianship. The flail has long associations with the gods Osiris, Min, and several sacred animals. Like the crook, it was one of the important insignias of royalty. Some scholars believe it to be a whip, maybe derived from a fly-whisk. Whilst others think it represents the '*ladanisterion*', an instrument used by very early goat herders. As such, the flail would symbolise past traditions and the shepherding aspects of Pharaoh's role as king. The ancient Egyptian name for a flail was '*nekhakha*'.

 Lotus: The sign for Rebirth and the emblem of Upper Egypt. Temple pillars often have lotus carved capitals. The lotus was symbolic of rebirth, since one of the creation myths describes how the newborn sun god rose out of a floating lotus. To celebrate this occurrence there was a hymn sung in the temple on festival days, the Lotus Offering, especially at the cult centre of Edfu. The blue lotus was also the emblem of the god Nefertem; 'The Lord of Perfume'. The lotus also appears to have been strongly connected with enjoyment and sensuality.

Obelisk: The word obelisk comes from the Greek word *obelos*, which means a pointed object. The Greeks in particular used the word to refer to the distinctive monuments of ancient Egypt. Obelisks were typically erected in pairs on the ceremonial way on either side of the entrance to a temple or tomb and it's thought that the monolith represented the primordial mound upon which the rays of the sun shone first. Egyptian obelisks were made from single blocks of red granite or similar rock, and the pyramidal top (pyramidion), most likely was sheathed in gold.

Pyramid: The pyramid is the symbol of Ascension. As a certain amount of astronomical observation was involved in the building of the pyramids, in particular the precise alignment with the cardinal points, it is believed the pyramid was a representation of the world's axis, with the body of the structure symbolising man's ascent to the heavenly skies - in particular, Pharaoh's ascension to Heaven and the Afterlife. It has also been proposed that the pyramid may have symbolised the sloping rays of the sun as a source of eternal strength and energy. Or it could have been designed to represent the Primeval Mound of Creation on which the sun-god was said to have been born.

Scarab: The sign of Resurrection. The scarab was a favourite amulet (charm) becoming associated with renewal and regeneration. It personified the god, Khepri, a sun god associated with resurrection. From the middle kingdom faineance scarabs were often used as a royal seal by pharaoh and would also be produced to celebrate certain events during his reign. There are various funerary types, for example, the large winged scarab and the heart scarab, which would be inserted within the linen wrapping during the mummification process.

 Sphinx: The sign of Wisdom and Protection. With a human head, body of a beast, the sphinx had access to all wisdom and strength and symbolised the riddle of human existence.

Egyptian Gods

 Amun: 'God of War' or the 'Hidden One'. A deity strongly associated with Thebes and Karnak Temple where he is described as 'the king of the gods'. He became assimilated with Ra, the most powerful sun god. There are many representations of Amun, including the Ram.

 Anubis: In primitive times Anubis, the jackal god, was associated with the dead because the jackal was generally seen prowling about the tombs. His worship is very ancient and may be older than that of Osiris. In the

Unas pyramid text (Book of the Dead) at Saqqara, he is associated with the Eye of Horus and his duty was that of guiding the dead through the underworld to Osiris. Again in the Funeral Procession scene Anubis receives the mummy and, standing by its bier, lays his protecting hands upon it. The duty of guiding the souls of the dead around the Underworld and into the kingdom of Osiris was shared by Anubis and another god, Ap-uat, whose symbol was also a jackal. Known as the Guardian of the Necropolis, he was also a patron of magic and it was believed he could foresee a person's destiny. Anubis was also the god of embalming and the keeper of poisons and medicines. It is written that he provided the ingredients (herbs, powders and unguents) to help Isis and Nephthys embalm Osiris. Anubis then performed the funeral of Osiris, which would be the role model for all funerals to come. As part of the funerary ritual he would perform the 'Opening of the Mouth' ceremony before the mummy was put into the tomb. This ensured that the deceased would be able to speak in the afterlife. In the "Hall of Maat", it is Anubis who sees that the beam of the great scale is in the proper position as he supervises the weighing of the heart of a deceased person against the feather of Maat to determine whether a person was good or evil. Anubis also protects the dead from Ammut, the 'Devourer'.

Hapi: This god was regarded as the 'Spirit or Essence of the Nile'. The annual inundation (flooding) was the arrival of Hapi. It was believed he had a cavern in the first cataract of the Nile at Aswan from where he discharged the rising waters. Along with Nephthys, his wife, Hapi guarded the canopic jar, which contained Pharaoh's lungs and whose stopper was the head of a baboon. He is often depicted as a well-fed man with a headdress of Nile plants.

Hathor: Goddess of Heaven, Earth and the Underworld. One of the most powerful goddesses she is often associated with Isis. She was known as Horus' wife. She had many titles, being closely associated with music, joy, the desert, and sexuality. Her cult was worshipped at Dendera and Memphis. She is often depicted as a cow, or a woman with ears of a cow, or a woman with wig, horns and sun disc.

 Horus: The 'Protector of the Reigning King'. The large impressive temples of Edfu and Komombo are dedicated to Horus. Known as the son of the god Osiris, he became known as the ancestor of all pharaohs. Pharaoh was known as 'Horus, the living God on Earth' Associated with both the sun and moon. He is usually depicted as a falcon or hawk.

 Isis: 'Goddess of Many Names' / 'Queen of the Gods'. Isis was the most popular Egyptian goddess, even though nothing is known of her origins. However, it is generally believed that she was worshipped in the Delta region, close to Busiris, the oldest known cult centre of Osiris. She had close associations with every great Egyptian goddess, including Nut, Bastet, and Hathor. Isis played a prominent role within the relationship of the gods. She was known as the daughter of Ged and Nut, the sister-wife of Osiris, the mother of Horus and the sister of Seth and Nephthys. She was also one of the four goddesses that guarded a corner of the royal sarcophagus. In her particular protection was Pharaoh's liver. Both Isis and Nephthys were known as the chief divine mourners at Pharaohs funeral.

But she is most famously known in mythology for her quest to find her murdered husband's body.

According to legend, Osiris was murdered by his evil brother Seth, who cut up his body and scattered it throughout Egypt. Isis then tirelessly searched until she had found all of her husband's body parts and using her powers brought Osiris back to life long enough for her to conceive their son, Horus. Osiris then adopted the role of 'God of the Underworld and Judge of the dead'. Horus later grew up to avenge his father's murder by defeating Seth in combat.

Throughout the legend of Osiris, Isis typified the faithful wife and devoted mother. Her magical powers, particularly in the care and cure of children, ensured her continuing popularity.

Isis took on particular importance during the Ptolemy reign (Dynasty XXX) when several temples were built in her honour including the temples at Dendera and Philae. The worship of Isis continued through both the Greek and Roman occupations of Egypt, up until the sixth century AD. During this time Isis was universally worshipped and her cult had spread through many lands including; Syria, Palestine, Asia, Cyprus, Crete, Rhodes, mainland Greece, Phoenicia and eventually Rome. The worship of Isis even spread as far as Britain. Isis is often depicted nursing her son Horus, or with wings, as on Tutankhamun's sarcophagus.

Min (Amun-Min): God of Fertility. As one of the most ancient of Egyptian gods he is probably predynastic. He is particularly associated with two ancient cities - Gebtu and Khent-Min where he was worshipped in the form of a white bull, a symbol of virility. As a desert deity he was also associated with nomads, travellers and hunters. Later, in the 18th dynasty he became linked with the most powerful of gods, Amun (Amun-Min). He had his own harvest celebration - 'The Festival of the Coming Forth of Min'.

Mut: Lady of Heaven. In the New Kingdom she acquired the position as a primeval goddess, called: "Mother of the Sun in Whom He rises". Mut was both the eye of the sun and the mother of the sun. The goddess was regarded as the mother of pharaohs. According to myth, she was self-created. She can be traced back to the Middle Kingdom, but was probably worshipped earlier. She was often depicted as a woman with a vulture skin on her head, together with the crown of Upper Egypt. Mut was also depicted as a woman standing with her arms stretched out with a large pair of wings. The goddess became the Eye of Ra when Amun was in the position of the sun god, and would often be represented as a lioness.

Osiris: Was the main god of the Underworld. The constant battles between Osiris and his brother, Seth, were the basis for the Egyptian account of the creation. The eventual death of Osiris, caused by this sibling struggle, enabled the Afterlife to come into being. As the principle god of the underworld and the judge of the dead, he represented order and justice in the next world and was the supreme ruler. It's thought that Osiris probably started out as a harvest god, due to his Atef crown. One of his principle cult centres was at Abydos. He wears the insignia of royalty with crook, flail and the Atef crown with plant stems and ostrich feathers.

Shu: God of Air and Light/ Guardian of the King / Supporter of the Heavens/ Son of Atum. He was popular in the New Kingdom and was usually associated with the sun god Ra. The main site of worship was at Nay-ta-but, South East of Heliopolis. He was usually depicted as a lion.

Historical Information

The Nile
The Nile has always been the backbone of Egypt. The mighty river flows for some 4,000 miles from the mountains of Equatorial Africa (Blue Nile) and Lake Victoria (White Nile) before it empties into the Mediterranean Sea. Without the Nile River and its annual inundation Ancient Egypt would never have come into being. Its fertile valley was renewed every year with rich silt deposits laid down during the flooding.

Nilometers were placed at various points along the Nile in order to monitor the changes in the water level. It was recorded that at the start of the flooding the clear waters would turn a turbid red.

As the agriculture of Egypt revolved around the Nile, so did the social life of the ancient Egyptians. During inundation when there was less to do, people had more time for recreational activities; they played games, held sporting tournaments and regularly feasted.

When the River Nile receded the appearance of the land had radically changed and there was a great rush to restore boundaries. There were many disputes as markers had moved, banks had collapsed, and distinguishable features had disappeared.

The river was also the chief means of transport. It was their highway, making roads superfluous, except between close villages. Virtually everything moved by boat.

The Nile, for the most part, is a gently flowing river and in the time of the ancients, was crammed with fish. It's easy flow made fishing very popular. Everyone enjoyed fishing, from the young to old, peasant to noble.

The Egyptians believed that the Nile was the centre of the world and the place from which it originated was, 'the beginning of the world'. In Lower Egypt, in the area of the Nile Delta, the river splits into two great arms. The area between the two was densely populated from the earliest times. Many of the major cult centres developed in this region. Even the soul of a deceased person had to cross the Nile before he could enter the 'Kingdom of the Dead'.

The ancients utilised every aspect of the river, and the achievements of both man and the Nile down the ages, deserves praise. The River Nile was the fundamental and protecting force of a great nation. Of all the great rivers, the Nile blessed its people with the most reliable and predictable cycle of seasons.

Extract from our Nile ebook:
http://www.ancientnile.co.uk/egyptian-ebook.php

Hatshepsut (18th Dynasty c.1473-1458 BC)
Hatshepsut was the daughter of Thutmose I. When Thutmose died his son Thutmose II succeeded him and, as was the custom, he married his stepsister, Hatshepsut. When Thutmose II also died, around 1479 BC, his son Thutmose III became Pharaoh. However as the new pharaoh was a minor, Hatshepsut stepped in as his regent.

Thutmose III and Hatshepsut ruled together until 1473 BC, when she eventually appointed herself Pharaoh. She did this by using a number of strategies to legitimise her role, including the claim that the god Amun-Ra had visited her mother while she was pregnant, which made her a divine child. She also readily assumed traditional kingly regalia, including several male attributes such as; a fake beard, male clothing, as well as having herself drawn and treated like a man.

During her fifteen-year reign she mounted at least one military campaign and initiated a number of impressive building projects, including her superb funerary temple at Deir al Bahri. One major achievement, the expedition to the Land of Punt, is shown on the temple walls. Believed to be located near the Red Sea, the drawings shows ebony, ivory, myrrh saplings, animal skins, gold, perfumes and exotic animals etc, being brought back from this Punt. Another remarkable achievement, also chronicled shows two huge granite obelisks being transported on the River Nile from Aswan to the Temple of Karnak.

Hatshepsut was a powerful and admirable woman who brought great stability to Egypt, however she mysteriously disappeared around 1458 BC, when Thutmose III regained his title as Pharaoh. It is thought the king despised Hatshepsut for keeping him from the throne and ordered all reference to her be wiped from Egyptian history. Hatshepsut's mummy has never been found and her name and images were nearly lost forever.

For more information on female pharaohs visit:
http://www.ancientnile.co.uk/pharaohs-women.php

Punt

The expedition is recorded on the walls of the Deir el Bahri temple and shows the wild and exotic creatures and plants that were successfully brought back to Egypt. It's believed that present day Ethiopia formed part of Punt. As early as 2500 BC, the Egyptian inscriptions indicate that they traded with people from the land of Punt, sometimes referring to it as 'God's Land'. To the Egyptian's Punt was a place of legend and fable. Ethiopia is old, even older than Egypt and is believed to be the very cradle of mankind with the remains of the earliest ancestral humans having been found there. To reach Punt the Egyptians sailed south along the Red Sea to trade for gold, ivory, exotic animals and incense.

Clothing

The ancient Egyptians costume, for the most part, was very simple and practical, consisting mainly of folded, pleated or draped linen. Sometimes other cultures would have an influence on their style, in particular; Assyria, Persia and at a much later date, Greece and Rome, but generally speaking the Egyptians remained true to their own designs, preferring their own scantier and lighter outfits. For over a period of three thousand years the changes in Egyptian dress were minimal.

Linens of various thickness were used to make clothing, the finest being semi-transparent gossamer-like linen, which was very much favoured by the Ancients. The beauty of linen was its versatility, in that it could be, stiffened, bleached, pleated, dyed, padded, embroidered etc. Egypt even had its own laundry industry in order to deal with the huge demands for cleaning, pressing, pleating etc.

Men generally wore white linen wrap-over kilts, or skirts, that reached anywhere from thigh to ankle. They were usually rectangular in shape and tied at the waist. Sometimes a band would also be worn and a piece added to form a sort of apron at the front. For the most part the men are usually shown bare-chested but sometimes they can be seen wearing a jerkin style top, most likely for warmth.

Extract from our Egyptian Dress ebook:
http://www.ancientnile.co.uk/egyptian-ebook.php

Cobra

The Cobra is the most feared of all poisonous snakes. Cobra De Capello is Portuguese for 'Hooded Snake'. At an average length of six feet, with a brownish skin, glaring eyes, darting tongue, hissing breath and spoon-shaped hood, it rates as one of the most dangerous snakes in the world.

It is a silent, stealthy hunter feeding on insects, lizards, frogs and small mammals, such as rats and mice. The Cobra snake favours warm, dry regions where water is readily available. As the cobra grows it sheds it skin.

The cobra's venom glands are essentially modified salivary glands, through which the cobra injects its victim. Even given its dangerous properties the Cobra still remains the favourite of snake charmers. Death from cobra snakebite is one of the oldest fates of mankind. In ancient Egypt every 'healer' was required to know the repertoire of spells for conjuring the poison of every serpent.

Pharaoh would often wear a representation of the wide hooded Cobra on his crown as an emblem of royalty. From this position the cobra was said to be able to defend the king.

In the 'Book of the Dead' the Cobra snake is seen as the symbol of Earth. Whilst the 'Ouroborus' a sign that shows a snake swallowing its own tail, brings together both circle and serpent - representing the round of existence.

Extract from our Cobra ebook:
http://www.ancientnile.co.uk/egyptian-ebook.php

Colossi of Memnon
Due to an earthquake in 27 BC, these statues were damaged and became known for a bell like tone that usually occurred in the morning due to rising temperatures and humidity. Unfortunately restoration work that was carried out during the time of the Roman Emperor Septemius Severus cured the statues of their 'singing'.

Each statue represents king Amenhotep III seated on his throne, wearing the Nemes or the royal headdress while the divine cobra is protecting his forehead. On the sides of the colossi there is a representation of the Nile god Hapi bending together the lotus and the papyrus plants, symbolizing the Union of Upper and Lower Egypt.

The Great Pyramid
The Great Pyramid is the most popular attraction in Egypt and was built for the Pharaoh Khufu (2589-2566BC - 4th Dynasty) The Greeks referred to Khufu as Cheops. It is

regarded as a 'true pyramid' having an angle just short of 52 degrees. Its original height was 146.6m. Its present height is 138.75m. Originally it had smooth sides, the stones having been covered with a limestone casing. Only the finest limestone, brought from the quarries at Tura was used for the outer casing that filled in the steps of the pyramid. Its base is 230 metres square and it has an estimated volume of 2,521,000 cubic metres. The pyramid contains a staggering 2.3 million blocks of stone, with an estimated weight of 6.5 million tonnes. The average weight of each stone is 2.5 tonnes but some weigh as much as 50 tonnes!

The stones were pulled on wooden sledges and it's thought that over 4000 skilled stonemasons worked on the pyramid. And, as reported by the Greek historian, Herodotus, possibly another 100,000 farmers joined them during the inundation period, (Annual flooding), when no farming was possible. However, the Egyptologist, Sir William Matthew Flinders Petrie thought a more realistic number would have been between five and six thousand.

Living quarters and workshops had to be specially built for the men and women. The workers were paid with food and drink rations. Approximately 100,000 bundles of onions and 200,000 loaves of bread were supplied daily to feed the workers three times a day. The workers received one day off in ten.

The burial chamber and inner passages are made of granite. The burial chamber ceiling consists of nine slabs of granite with a combined weight of approximately 400 tonnes. This granite was shipped from quarries at Aswan, some 800 kilometres (500 miles) away. The pyramid took over 20 years to complete, but prior to this, it took ten years to prepare the ground, waterways, underground chambers, ramps etc. The Great Pyramid is arguably the most accomplished engineering feat of the Ancient World.

For more information on pyramids visit:
http://www.ancientnile.co.uk/pyramids.php

Egyptian Food

The Ancient land of Egypt was one of the most fertile valleys in the world and supported one of the world's greatest civilisations. Rich soil, provided by the river's annual flooding, deposited thick silt over the land providing sometimes two, or even three, harvests a year. Herodotus, a famous Greek historian, once wrote that Egypt was the Gift of the Nile.

Bread was the staple diet of most Egyptians and usually made from barley. The average kitchen was commonly situated at the rear of the house, or on the roof. Mostly it was in the open, but may have been partially shaded. Egyptian food was cooked in simple clay pots, using wooden utensils and stored in jars.

Beer was the national drink and was also made from barley. To improve the taste the Egyptians would add spices and it was usually stored in labelled clay jars. The importance of beer to the ancient Egyptians should not be underestimated as it was esteemed so highly that it was regularly offered as libation to the gods. Wine for the upper classes was made from local vineyards. After the harvest was gathered, the workers would tread the grapes, and the juice collected. Other wines were made from pomegranates or plums.

Even the poor people of Ancient Egypt ate a fairly healthy diet including vegetables, fruit and fish. But it was only the larger plantations that grazed animals, mainly because the average farmer had to use his limited land to grow crops. Poultry was mostly roasted for the table, but meat was mainly the privilege of the rich. Seasoning included salt, pepper, cumin, coriander, sesame, dill, fennel, fenugreek, seeds etc.

All of the big festivals of the year were religious and organised by the temple priests. The biggest of these was the festival of the god Amun that lasted a whole month. Music, dancers, singers, acrobats and jugglers would accompany the religious procession. Much feasting and partying went on with a great deal of wine and beer being consumed. There would be; music, singing, story telling and the younger members of the family would dance to entertain the guests.

Although the ancient people did not write down their recipes, or use cook books, the ingredients needed to make most of the dishes are well known, many of which are still used in Egypt today.

Extract from our Egyptian Diet ebook:
http://www.ancientnile.co.uk/egyptian-ebook.php

The Great Sphinx
The sphinx is a mystical beast portrayed with the head of a man and the body of a lion. It is shown wearing the royal head cloth. (Nemes) The ancient Greek word sphinx means; strangler. The Arabs call it, 'Abu Hol', meaning; The Father of Terror. However some believe that the name may come from the Egyptian phrase 'shesep ankh', which means living image.

The Great Sphinx sits in front of the pyramid of Khafra, next to the funerary causeway. And its face probably represents the 4th Dynasty ruler. However, other scholars believe it is older, dating back to the reign of Khufu. Whilst some even believe it may be 10,000 years old.

The sphinx is associated with both pharaoh and the sun-god, Ra. And is considered to be the Guardian of the Necropolis of Giza. It measures 73m long and has a maximum height of 20m. The Sphinx has no markings (epigraphic documentation) to help date it. It was carved from a single knoll of stone, probably what was left behind after quarrying.

It has been buried by sand on several occasions and has had to be uncovered. One such incident is recorded on the 'Dream Stele', which stands between the paws of the Sphinx. This tells how Prince Tuthmoses (1400-1390 BC) described how in a dream he was promised that if he cleared the Sphinx of sand, he would become King. He became Tuthmoses IV. Much reconstruction work has been carried out on the sphinx in the form of limestone cladding.

The gradual deterioration of the sphinx, caused by increased humidity, water infiltration and air pollution, has caused much concern. Over the years, the sphinx has lost its nose, royal beard, cobra emblem, and various other pieces of masonry. Further damage was done when the Mameluke and Napoleonic troops used it for target practice.

In ancient times the Sphinx would have been brightly coloured. Remains of the dyes can be seen on the side of its face. The Sphinx, in the New Kingdom, was also identified with 'Horem akhet', Horus in the Horizon'. (Horus is often seen as the son of Ra.)

Herodotus, the Greek historian, never mentions the Great Sphinx when recording his travels in Egypt, most likely because at the time the Sphinx was once again covered by sand. The most comprehensive exploration of the sphinx was carried out by Giovanni Battista Caviglia in 1816. He discovered fragments of the royal beard, which were given to the British Museum. The Sphinx faces east. The Sphinx plays the role of narrator in the Sound and Light shows that are performed every evening for tourists. Three tunnels have been discovered in the Sphinx, behind the head, in its tail and in its north side. None lead anywhere.

For more information on the Sphinxes visit:
http://www.ancientnile.co.uk/sphinx.php

Mummification

The first mummies in Egypt were preserved naturally when the deceased was buried in the desert sands. This enabled desiccation (drying out) to take place. Bodily fluids would seep into the sand and what remained namely; skin, hair, tendons and ligaments, would dry out naturally. Other ways that bodies have been preserved around the world are; ice, sunlight, smoke, fire, chemicals, peat bogs, certain soils and mud.

The ancient Egyptians believed that to enjoy the Afterlife, the body of the deceased should bear as close a resemblance to the living person as possible. Features of the face were often modelled in linen bandages and painted. Even nipples and the male sex organs have been found modelled in cloth and placed in position so the deceased would be entire in the afterlife.

When graves became more elaborate and the deceased were no longer just buried in the desert, the ancient Egyptians found that the bodies started to decay. Which was the complete opposite to what they strived for. So, they started to look for ways to emulate, by artificial means, the preserving properties of the sand graves. By the first dynasty there is evidence that natron, a natural salt found in Egypt, was being used. The body would be covered in the salt, which acted like the hot desert sand and started the process of desiccation. However using natron alone proved not to be enough, as bodies would still decompose due to internal organs.

Evisceration (disembowelling) was the next stage of development in mummification, which involved removing the internal organs so the moisture they contained did not cause internal rotting of the corpse. Removal of the brain was done through the nose, using a pick. The heart was left in place, as the Egyptians believe it housed the person's soul. Removed body organs would be wrapped in linen, coated in resin and laid close by, either in a recess, or in later dynastic periods, in four canopic jars. This was to ensure that the deceased would still be whole in the afterlife. The entire body was covered in many layers of linen, impregnated with resin to try and keep out the elements. However it was eventually realised that the decaying process started from within the body and not by the outside elements. The quality of the linen used to wrap the mummy varied according to the quality of the mummification. The reams and reams of bandages gave shape to the dried out corpses.

It is believed that the word 'mummy' comes from the Arabic word 'mummiya' meaning bitumen - a tar-like substance. This is because when early Arabs saw mummies, which were covered in black resin, they thought that the ancients had used bitumen. Immortality depended upon the mummification of the body, as it also preserved the 'Ka' - the spirit that accompanied the physical body in life. If the body decayed so did the person's 'Ka' spirit. The New Kingdom (18th - 20th dynasties 1600 - 1050 BC) produced some of the best-preserved mummies.

For more information on mummification visit:
http://www.ancientnile.co.uk/mummy.php

The Royal Harem

In the private sections of the Royal Household were quarters devoted purely to the women of the Palace, including the first Queen, lesser wives and concubines. The ancient Egyptian word, which commonly referred to this part of the Palace, was *ipet* or *per-khemret*, which is often translated into, 'harem'. It would perhaps be more accurate to translate *ipet* or *per-khemret* into 'private rooms or apartments', as opposed to the more public parts of a Palace where business was carried out.

Presiding over all proceedings of the household would be the first queen, who was most likely to be of Royal birth, sometimes a half or full sister to Pharaoh. She would have also been a woman of considerable personal wealth, influence, and, as the wife of the living god on earth, highly privileged.

Surviving texts describe 'harems' as important economic organisations that received regular supplies of rations and were governed very much as a business. They were obviously powerful and independent establishments, both physically and economically, and it is not surprising that occasionally they would become involved in political intrigue.

One account of 'harem treachery' involved the Pharaoh Ramses III (1184-1153 BC). It was devised by one of his lesser wives, Tiye who planned to dispose of the king before installing her son onto the throne. The details of the trial have been handed down nearly complete in the Judicial Papyrus of Turin, which was translated by M. Le Page Renouf. The fate of Tiye is not recorded on the surviving papyri but it is known that many were forced to commit suicide. It is obvious that the Egyptian queens royal harem was an integral part of the palace's economy, stability and sometimes a place of serious intrigue.

Extract from our Harem ebook:
http://www.ancientnile.co.uk/egyptian-ebook.php

Egyptian Sexuality

Long before the Greek and Roman artists depicted and described the most intimate aspects of human behaviour the ancient Egyptians had been practising their sensual expression for centuries. Erotica flowed through all levels of society like the waters of the Nile and although the evidence is scarcer it is no less potent. Ancient Egyptians believed that life, sexuality and rebirth were elements that went hand in hand. Marriage seems to have been a voluntary affair and for the most part monogamous - mainly because polygamy, whilst not illegal, was expensive. Adultery was considered a serious crime and carried severe punishments including the cutting off of the nose.

The reputation of Egyptians as an incestual race is not a strictly deserved one. Although there are clear cases of royal families marrying close relatives it must be understood that this was done to secure the royal blood line and preserve peace and legitimacy, rather than for debauched reasons.

Love poems and erotic texts are numerous and it is obvious that the ancient Egyptian man was not afraid of demonstrating his love. He speaks through tales of gods, poetry, dreams and books of wisdom.

Cleanliness and ornamentation were all important to the Egyptians. They would wash daily and both sexes removed unwanted hair from their bodies. Women curled their hair and shadowed their eyes. The ancient Egyptians were a people comfortable with their sensuality and undoubtedly loved and celebrated life to the full.

Extract from our Egyptian Sexuality ebook:
http://www.ancientnile.co.uk/egyptian-ebook.php

Egyptian Hieroglyphs

On this page you will find the common signs and symbols used by the artisans and scribes of the temples.

Depending upon which book you are referring to, you may find there are various hieroglyphs for different letters - sometimes even two or three.

Below we have given, what we consider, to be the most popular.

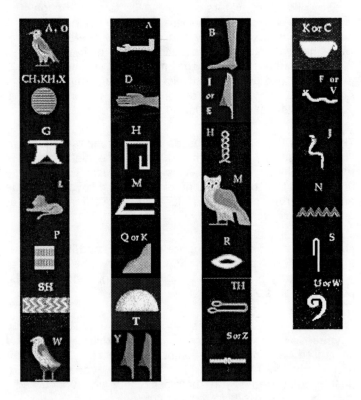

The Arabic Language

History
The official language of Egypt is Egyptian Arabic. As the language of the Quran, the holy book of Islam, Arabic is widely understood throughout the Muslim world. Today over 150 million people speak Arabic and it is the official language of 18 countries. Some 50 million people speak Egyptian Arabic.

Arabic was originally the language of the nomadic Bedouin in the North Arabian Desert and has its origins in the Semitic language, which is closely related to Hebrew. The Arabic alphabet is believed to have evolved from that of an ancient people known as the Nabateans. Then, in the seventh century when the Muslims conquered much of the Middle East and North Africa Arabic displaced the native language in many countries, including Coptic in Egypt.

Structure:
The Arabic alphabet consists of 28 consonants and three vowels (a, i, u), which can be short or long. Some of the sounds are unique to Arabic and difficult for non-native speakers to pronounce correctly, though you should be able to make yourself understood.

Arabic sentences are usually written from right to left and the normal structure of a sentence is verb-subject-object. Nouns are inflected and marked for case, gender (masculine and feminine), number (singular, plural, dual and collective) and determination (definite and indefinite). Arabic has very few irregular verbs and does not use "is" or "are". For example 'busy the man' means 'the man is busy'.

Useful Arabic Words

You can find some of these words spoken on our website at
www.ancientnile.co.uk/eb-links/words.php

1	wahed
2	etnien
3	talata
4	arbaa
5	khamsa
6	sitta
7	sabaa
8	thamania
9	tesaa
10	ashara
20	eshreen
21	wahed eshreen
22	etnien whe eshreen
50	khamsin
100	mia
500	khams mia
1000	elf

Airport mattar
Bathroom hammam
Beer beera
Big kabier
Beautiful gamil
Chicken dajaaj
Coffee ahua
Daughter bint
Doctor doctur
Eat yacol
Emergency tawarek
Fish samak
Food akal
Fork showka
Full maliin
God Willing inshaalha
Gold dahab
Goodbye ma'a'salam / Salam (peace)
Good Evening masa el-kheir
Good Morning sabah el-kheir
Good Night tesbah ala kheir
Go away imshe
How much? bekam
I don't understand ana mish fahem
I want ariyad or aawez
Is it far? hal bieat

It's Too Expensive ghali awi
knife sikkiyn
Leave me alone sebni fi haelee
Little shoeya
Long tawiel
Marketplace souk
Milk halib
Money feluus
Museum mat-hhaf
My name is ana ismee
Never mind maalish
No la (or la'a)
No, I don't have laa ma audich
No, thank you La'a shukran
Now delwakty
Open maftah
Outside barra
Pharmacy sighdaliya
Please min fadlak (male) min fadlik (Female)
Possible mumken
Restaurant mataam
Salt malh
Sleep noum
Slowly shwai
Sorry / Excuse me assef
Soup shurba
Station mahatta
Sugar sokkar
Thank you shukran
That's Fine/Perfect tamam
Tea shay
Telephone teliphune
Ticket tazkara
Town medina
Vegetables khudra
Water mayya
Welcome marhaba
What is this eh dah?
What do you call this in arabic? maza tosumi haza bel arabi?
Where fein
Where Can I Buy...? fein mumken ashtari...?
Wine nebite
Yes aywa,(Luxor) naam (Cairo)

Books in the Travel Egypt Series:

1. Nile Cruise: Ever wondered what happens on a Nile cruise? Then this book is for you. As well as describing a typical cruise schedule it also tells you 'how it really is'. This is done by not over romanticising the experience, as most brochures do, but by offering you sound and practical advice. The book contains useful bartering tips, how to deal with hassle or unwanted attention, medical information, anecdotes, hints and tips, Arabic phrases, reviews, safety issues and much more. It also provides general information on such things as, money matters, boat facilities, local dishes, clothing, meals, drinks, local customs, entertainment and those extra costs travel agents rarely tell you about! This book is a must read for any of you thinking of taking a Nile cruise as it contains information you will be hard pressed to find in one place!

2. Around Luxor: This book goes through what you can expect from a hotel-based holiday in Luxor. It covers many aspects including some of the best places to eat, ways to get around Luxor and surrounding area, medical advice, local scams / tricks, useful tips, in depth detail on balloon trips over the Valley of the Kings, local ancient sites, plus hotel and town facilities. The book also has a section dealing with some of the main hotels regularly used by travel companies. These include; the Jolie Villa Movenpick, Luxor Sheraton, Isis Pyramid, Le Meridian, Sonesta St George, Novotel, Old Winter Palace, New Winter Palace, Mercure Etap and Luxor Hilton – with exterior and interior shots wherever possible. If you are looking for information regarding; arrival, travel visa, welcome meeting, health issues, local con-tricks, transport, toilet facilities then this book is a must.

3. Photographing the Ancient Sites: A travel book that gives you hints and tips on how and what to photograph whilst on your Egyptian holiday or Nile cruise. The book is illustrated throughout with our own photography. It contains a list of handy hints, various links, advantage points and personal suggestions. It also includes what film types are best, what to avoid and the minimum equipment you may need. It offers advice on the ancient sites such as Karnak and Luxor Temples, the Pyramids and tombs. It also discusses digital usage, plus image manipulation and creativity with computer software such as Photoshop.

4. Three Books in One: This unique package incorporates all the above three books. All these books have been put together from our own photographic collection, experiences and personal observations. To read more go to: www.ancientnile.co.uk/egyptian-books.php

ETERNAL RIVER by STEVEN WOOD

Music to sail the Nile by

If you are also looking for some 'special music' to listen to during your Egyptian holiday then I would suggest our 'Eternal River CD which is available from our website at http://www.ancientnile.co.uk/egyptian-music.php.

Here you can listen to samples, download a demo, order the CD or download the music for use with your mp3 / iPod player.

The CD includes the following songs

Eternal River: Let yourself drift away on the Eternal River as you listen to the babbling water and the gentle sound of a soothing breeze. The sounds of nature are the perfect complement to this very unique music as the ethereal, whispering sounds transport you back in time.

Desert March: This music is a throwback to the Golden Era of film. For example, this song would not be out of place in a epic type of movie. The Neo-Classical style of this song is created by the impressive orchestral sounds.

Cobra: The fabled Cobra of ancient Egypt was the royal snake of the Pharaohs. She was said to protect the king by spitting venom and flames at his enemies. Listen to the serpent as she stalks her prey. 'Cobra' has an Arabic 'eastern promise' quality.

Exodus: It is quite easy to imagine yourself crossing the deserts and plains with Moses as he triumphantly leads his people out of Egypt to the sounds of trumpets. Another impressive orchestral piece.

Tears of Isis: A haunting Egyptian melody about the tears that Isis shed following the brutal death of her husband, Osiris. Her tears are said to fill the Nile River.

World of Anubis: Listen to our tribute to the Ancient Egyptian Lord of the Underworld, Anubis (god of all mummification). Let its eerie and mystical sound carry you into the dark realm of the mysterious world of the dead.

Hall of Whispers: This music was inspired by a visit to the mysterious and shadowy Festival Hall. If you listen carefully you may just hear the priests whispers amongst the sounds of the dancers sistrums. A romantic and mesmerizing flute music that has a very unique style and sound which is further enhanced by the soothing tones of strings and mysterious whispering vocals.

Treachery: A dynamic and dramatic song with a rhythmic hard beat. Hear the full power of the orchestra. The 'Harem Treachery', which involved the stabbing of Pharaoh Ramses III, was the inspiration behind this song. You can almost imagine the perpetrator committing the act and then hiding away in the deep shadows of the palace. This music is both powerful and emotive.

Immortal Spirit: The Ka spirit is the vital force of divine creative power and the forces of continuity. It bridges the gap between the living and the dead and the Spirit of the Soul. Listen to the sounds of piano and haunting flute that will take you on a calm and peaceful journey.

This Ancient Egyptian inspired music has been especially written for Ancient Nile and at present is only available from www.ancientnile.co.uk. I listen to it whenever I'm cruising the Nile, or relaxing around the pool, as it constantly inspires me to write, or imagine what life must have been like during the time of the Pharaohs.

Internet Links

Other books in this Travel Egypt Series: Around Luxor and Photographing the Ancient Sites (Special Offer):
http://www.ancientnile.co.uk/eb-links/discount.php

UK and USA Travel Companies
http://www.ancientnile.co.uk/eb-links/uk-us-travel.php

Travel Books - Tour guides and Maps
http://www.ancientnile.co.uk/eb-links/travel.php

Phrase Books - Ideal for Tourists
http://www.ancientnile.co.uk/eb-links/arabic.php

Egyptian Fiction - Ideal holiday reading
http://www.ancientnile.co.uk/eb-links/fiction.php

Egyptian Music CD
http://www.ancientnile.co.uk/egyptian-music.php

Egyptian Multimedia (Movies, Videos, Music etc)
http://www.ancientnile.co.uk/eb-links/multimedia-index.php

Arabic Language Courses
http://www.ancientnile.co.uk/eb-links/arabic2.php

Belly Dance (Music, DVD, Books, Video)
http://www.ancientnile.co.uk/eb-links/bellydance.php

Egyptian Gifts and Items on Ebay
http://www.ancientnile.co.uk/eb-links/ebay.php

Downloadable Freebies
http://www.ancientnile.co.uk/eb-links/freebies.php

Fun and Games
http://www.ancientnile.co.uk/eb-links/fun.php

Cheap Travel Insurance (most countries)
http://www.ancientnile.co.uk/eb-links/travel-insurance.php

Airport Parking UK
http://www.ancientnile.co.uk/eb-links/airport-parking.php

Transport to UK Airports
http://www.ancientnile.co.uk/eb-links/airport-transport.php

General Travel Information (Medical, Currency, Site list etc)
http://www.ancientnile.co.uk/eb-links/travel-index.php

Money Converter
http://www.ancientnile.co.uk/eb-links/converter.php

Official and Egyptian Facts Websites
British Embassy in Egypt
http://www.britishembassy.org.eg/

UK Foreign Office: Tourist Advice
http://www.fco.gov.uk/

US Embassy in Egypt
http://www.usembassy.egnet.net/

US Dept of State: Travel Advice
http://travel.state.gov/travel/egypt.html

Terrorist Attacks in Egypt
http://www.usdivetravel.com/T-EgyptTerrorism.html

Egypt - A country study
http://lcweb2.loc.gov/frd/cs/egtoc.html

World Fact Book: Egypt
http://www.cia.gov/cia/publications/factbook/geos/eg.html

Egyptian Marriage Requirements
http://marriage.about.com/od/international/p/egypt.htm

INDEX

Money Conversion Chart

The chart below should only be used as a rough guide as the exchange rate constantly alters. Before leaving for Egypt remember to check for current rates.

EGYPT (LE)	UK (£)	US ($)	CANADA ($)	EUROPE (EURO)	AUSTRALIA ($)
1	0.10	0.18	0.21	0.15	0.25
5	0.50	0.90	1.05	0.75	1.25
10	1.00	1.80	2.10	1.50	2.50
15	1.50	2.70	3.15	2.25	3.75
20	2.00	3.60	4.20	3.00	5.00
35	3.50	6.30	7.35	5.25	8.75
50	5.00	9.00	10.50	7.50	12.50
75	7.50	13.50	15.75	11.25	18.75
100	10.00	18.00	21.00	15.00	25.00

Egyptian Exchange Rate History for the UK

01/01/04	10.012
01/01/05	10.774
01/01/06	9.675

Notes

Notes

LaVergne, TN USA
03 January 2009
168728LV00001B/11/A